A Bookman's Fantasy

How Science Fiction Became Respectable, and Other Essays

Twenty-four essays by
Fred Lerner

with
four introductions

NESFA Press
Post Office Box 809
Framingham, Massachusetts
01701-0203

ISBN: 0-915368-65-X
Library of Congress Catalog Number 94-73980
Fantasy Collection Classification Scheme PX320.L395

First Edition: February 1995

Introductions to the four sections, copyright © 1995 by Fred Lerner
How Science Fiction Became Respectable, copyright © 1995 by Fred Lerner
Lester and Me, copyright © 1993 by Fred Lerner (*Lofgeornost* #32, Aug. 1993)
Towards a Definition of Science Fiction: A Reply to James Gunn, copyright © 1986 by Fred Lerner (*Lofgeornost* #8, Nov. 1986)
"A Master of Our Art," copyright © 1993 by Fred Lerner (*Voice of Youth Advocates,* Oct. 1993)
Reading About Robert Heinlein, copyright © 1981 by Fred Lerner (*Niekas* #27, Aug. 1981)
What I Did on My Vacation, copyright © 1994 by Fred Lerner (*Niekas* #44, Mar. 1994)
The Posthumous Heinlein, copyright © 1994 by Fred Lerner (*Voice of Youth Advocates,* Apr. 1994)
"The Horror! The Horror!," copyright © 1995 by Fred Lerner (*Niekas* #45, forthcoming)
1994 Revisited, copyright © 1994 by Fred Lerner (*Lofgeornost* #36, Aug. 1994)
Concerning Purely Personal Preferences, copyright © 1984 by Fred Lerner (*Voice of Youth Advocates* Oct. 1994)
The Science Fiction Library, copyright © 1973 by Fred Lerner (*Special Libraries,* Jan. 1973)
The Cataloging and Classification of Science Fiction Collections, copyright © 1983 by Fred Lerner (*Special Collections,* 1983)
The Popularity of Science Fiction, copyright © 1982 by Fred Lerner (*Voice of Youth Advocates,* Oct. 1982)
Farewell to Alexandria, copyright © 1992 by Fred Lerner (*Lofgeornost* #26, Feb. 1992)
Vermonting, copyright © 1994 by Fred Lerner (*Lofgeornost* #36, Aug.1994)
Proceedings and Transactions of the Vermont Commission on Tackiness, copyright © 1994 by Fred Lerner (*Lofgeornost* #36, Aug. 1994)
Uncle Bounce, I'll Miss You, copyright © 1993 by Fred Lerner (*Lofgeornost* #32, Aug. 1993)
An Evening with Richard Snelling, copyright © 1982 by Fred Lerner (*Lofgeornost* #4, Nov. 1982)
The Vermont Bicentennial, copyright © 1995 by Fred Lerner
A Desert Island Dozen, copyright © 1979 by Fred Lerner (*Lofgeornost* #1, Aug. 1979)
A Goliard Christmas, copyright © 1980 by Fred Lerner (*Niekas* #22, 1980)
A Day in the Commonwealth, copyright © 1988 by Fred Lerner (*Niekas* #37, Aug. 1988)
All Aboard!..., copyright © 1982 by Fred Lerner (*Niekas* #29, Feb. 1982)
Sherlock Holmes in India, copyright © 1986 by Fred Lerner (*Lofgeornost* #8, Nov. 1986)

Dedication

To Elizabeth, who shares a bookman's fantasy

Contents

Science Fiction, Respectable and Otherwise

A Librarian Born and Bred

An Imperfect Vermonter

A Bookman's Fantasy

Science Fiction, Respectable and Otherwise

I think that the first science fiction book I ever read was *Miss Pickerel Goes to Mars*. But it was television shows such as *Tom Corbett, Space Cadet* and *Rod Brown and the Rocket Rangers* that made the strongest impression on my young mind. (I still remember the Saturday morning spent peering from behind a good stout chair, hiding from the wrath of the Stick-Men of Neptune.) As a seven-year-old in day camp I wrote a brief SF story, short on plot but abundantly supplied with unpronounceable alien names. It was published in the camp newspaper, the *Vernon Journal*; fortunately no copies survive.

I never outgrew my interest in science fiction, and read it steadily through high school and college. In December 1962, a chance encounter with one of its more colorful members in a Columbia College dormitory led me to join the Evening Session Science Fiction Society at nearby City College. Even had I not met Carl Frederick, I would doubtless have become involved with Fandom. I knew of its existence, and had even acquired a copy of *The Eighth Stage of Fandom*; this collection of Robert Bloch's fan writing made me want to learn more. My main extracurricular activity at Columbia was WKCR-FM, the student radio station. I worked as assistant producer for *The Printed Word*, editing taped interviews with leading writers. I was allowed to conduct two interviews myself, and I chose *Analog* editor John Campbell and SF historian Sam Moskowitz as my guests. Had I not been involved in Fandom by then I'm sure one of these gentlemen would have steered me in the right direction. Later in my WKCR career I got to produce my own program, a monthly series called *Exploring Science Fiction* on which I interviewed Randall Garrett, Frederik Pohl, and James Blish, among others. So far as I know *Exploring Science Fiction* was the first regular program about science fiction in American broadcasting.

After college (I graduated in 1966) and two years in the Army. I returned to Columbia for library school. This I enjoyed enough to return for more; after three years of working as a librarian, I entered the doctoral program at the School of Library Service.

My dissertation on science fiction's changing reputation in America was accepted by Columbia University, and I earned the D.L.S. in 1981. "How Science Fiction Became Respectable" is a talk I gave at ConStellation (the 41st World Science Fiction Convention, which was held at Baltimore in 1983) in which I summarized my findings. A revised and expanded version of my study was later published as *Modern Science Fiction and the American Literary Community* (Metuchen, New Jersey: Scarecrow Press, 1985).

Although Columbia had encouraged me to write a dissertation on science fiction, I had to undergo the usual academic obstacles. My path was a bit easier than it might have been because I had an unusual champion on my examining committee. "Lester and Me" first appeared in *Lofgeornost* #32 (August 1993), a personal fanzine I produce for the Fantasy Amateur Press Association.

At ConFederation (the 44th World Science Fiction Convention, Atlanta, 1986) I was invited to participate in a program on "Defining Science Fiction." James Gunn proposed a definition of the genre, which David Hartwell and I critiqued. So far as I know neither Gunn's presentation nor Hartwell's response has been published. Mine appeared in *Lofgeornost* #8 (November 1986).

In 1990 I began writing a column for *Voice of Youth Advocates*, a magazine for librarians working with adolescents. My goal was to give my readers some idea of important trends in the science fiction field, and my editors gave me free rein to choose those aspects of fantasy and science fiction I would discuss. I took the opportunity offered by John Brunner's compilation of two collections of Rudyard Kipling stories to describe my favorite writer's influence on modern science fiction. " 'A Master of Our Art' " appeared in the October 1993 issue.

Like many fans of my generation, I was attracted to science fiction largely by the stories of Robert A. Heinlein; and, like many of my contemporaries, my admiration for his writing came to be tempered by the realization that both as a storyteller and as an ideologue Heinlein's work was seriously flawed. I've read practically everything that Heinlein has published, and I've also read most of what has been published about him. In "Reading About Robert Heinlein," which first appeared in *Niekas* #27 (August 1981), I examined the biographical and critical writing about Heinlein that had been published up to then. After Heinlein died in 1988, books from his hand continued to appear. "What I Did on My Vacation," originally published in *Niekas* #44 (March 1994), and "The Posthumous Heinlein" (*Voice of Youth Advocates*, April 1994) are my responses to these additions to the Heinlein canon.

My "Across the River" column appears regularly in Ed Meskys's fanzine *Niekas*, and when Ed devotes an issue to a special topic I try to shape my piece accordingly. I wasn't sure what sort of contribution I'd be able to make to an issue on horror fiction, until I thought to use it as an opportunity to examine my distaste for horror. "The Horror! The Horror!" appears in *Niekas* #45 (in press).

In 1984 the editors of *Voice of Youth Advocates* asked me to write an article on "George Orwell and Modern Science Fiction: The Legacy of Big Brother" (which appeared in *VOYA*'s April 1984 issue). I found that *Nineteen Eighty-Four* didn't really have much of an influence on the field; "Big Brother died intestate," I concluded. But one SF story influenced by Orwell's vision had appeared back in 1969, and on the twenty-fifth anniversary of its publication I thought it might be interesting to reread it and see how *Teg's 1994* differed from our own. This piece appeared in *Lofgeornost* #36 (August 1994).

In the spring of 1994 I left *Voice of Youth Advocates* to begin writing the monthly "Science Fiction Multiverse" column for the *Wilson Library Bulletin*. I bade my *VOYA* readers farewell with an evocation of my favorite books. "Concerning Purely Personal Preferences" appeared in the October 1994 issue.

How Science Fiction Became Respectable

There was a time, not so very long ago, when science fiction was something to be ashamed of. Its readers hid the garish covers of their pulp magazines, and its writers earned little money and less recognition from their work. Science fiction was banned from the classroom, unwelcome in the library, ignored by the literary establishment. But times have changed.

Science fiction has become big business. There are quite a few SF writers whose earnings from science fiction place them in the top few percentiles in American earnings statistics. There are many more whose science fiction writing provides a healthy supplement to the income they earn in more conventional occupations. And there is an enormous branch of the entertainment industry in this country devoted to the merchandising of science fiction in one form or another.

Back in 1939, a World Science Fiction Convention meant two hundred people—mostly young men in their teens and twenties—gathering in a shabby fourth-floor meeting room. Today a major SF convention brings almost ten thousand people to luxury hotels and downtown convention centers.

How did this state of affairs come into being? How was science fiction transformed, in the eyes of the American public, from a despised subcategory of the least reputable form of commercial fiction, to a literary genre published by the most prestigious American presses, studied in this country's leading universities, and read by millions of the brightest and most literate American readers?

When we talk about the origins of science fiction, there's a temptation to begin at the very origins of literature itself. Various historians have claimed the *Epic of Gilgamesh*, the Hindu mythology, the Book of Ezekiel, Homer's *Odyssey*, and almost any other ancient story that included a fantastic episode, as a direct ancestor to modern science fiction. But there's little point in grafting such illustrious ancestors onto science fiction's family tree. We're *all* descended from Adam, so why carry our literary genealogy to preposterous extremes?

It's more sensible to begin the history of science fiction in the 19th century. Brian Aldiss suggests Mary Shelley's *Frankenstein* as the first true science fiction story. Others have claimed that Edgar Allan Poe was "father of the genre." And there are, of course, many who think of Jules Verne as the inventor of science fiction. Certainly, by the end of the 19th century, a lot of science fiction had been published in the most respectable American and British magazines. Such writers as Nathaniel Hawthorne, Herman Melville, and Mark Twain in the United States, and Rudyard Kipling and Sir Arthur Conan Doyle across the Water, wrote science fiction for these publications; and the novels of H. G. Wells were popular on both sides of the Atlantic.

But let us remember something. These stories and novels on scientific themes were accepted by editors and readers simply as stories. There was no notion of a special type of literature in which they might be classified, and therefore no question of the respectability of science fiction: for all practical purposes, neither the term nor even the concept existed until several decades later.

So stories based on science and technology existed and flourished, but only as one current in the literary mainstream. Meanwhile, there were some interesting developments in another literary environment, in what we might call the "underground river" that paralleled the mainstream of "respectable" literature.

Until the beginning of the 19th century, reading was primarily an activity of the middle and upper classes of society. Working people had little education, and less time, for reading. But the growth of public school systems, and the invention of labor-saving machinery—and better artificial lighting—created a new audience for pleasure reading. The mechanization of printing and transportation made the production of inexpensive reading matter possible, and indeed lucrative. And there's one other factor to be considered. Somewhere around 1820, a process was invented for making cheap paper out of wood-pulp. Remember that word: "pulp" plays a big part in our story.

So, by the middle of the 19th century, millions of Americans were reading story papers—these were all-fiction magazines printed in newspaper format, to qualify for cheap postal rates; the history of popular literature in this country has always been more a matter of economics than of aesthetics—and these story papers evolved into inexpensive paperbacks published in series (again with an eye on postal costs). Such paperbacks came to be called "dime novels," and they were read, in the words of historian Merle Curti, "by almost everyone except schoolma'ams, pedants, and the illiterate."

The Steam Man of the Prairies was the first dime novel known to use a scientific theme. It was published in 1868, and as its title suggests, it can be regarded as one of the earliest robot stories. By 1892, this primitive SF was so popular that one publisher brought out a series consisting entirely of this sort of thing. Sam Moskowitz tells us that this *Frank Reade Library* was "the first regular periodical completely devoted to science fiction."

At about this time a new type of periodical publication was emerging. Frank Munsey found that there was a niche for an inexpensive magazine devoted to short stories and serialized novels; and *Munsey's Magazine* and its companion, *Argosy*, enjoyed a wide circulation. They cost the same ten-cent price as the dime novels; and by 1920, the so-called "pulp magazines" had pretty well replaced the dime novel as the leading newsstand source of popular fiction. Specialized titles began to appear: *Detective Story Magazine*, *Western Story Magazine*, even *Zeppelin Stories*!

So in 1926, when Hugo Gernsback decided to publish a magazine consisting entirely of "scientifiction" stories (as he called them), there already was an industry devoted to publishing and distributing all-fiction periodicals aimed at a special-interest audience. If one publisher successfully introduced a new type of magazine for a new type of audience, competing publishers would launch imitations of their own. Magazine distributors and newsstand operators knew what to do with a new type of all-fiction magazine. They put it next to the westerns and the detective stories. And the American literary establishment knew what to do with a new type of all-fiction magazine. They ignored it.

Neither the pulp magazines nor their literary predecessors had any cultural pretensions. The editor of Street & Smith's *Popular Magazine*, a general-fiction pulp, considered his publication to be "a place of entertainment whence comes amusement and diversion and thorough enjoyment." A worthwhile enterprise, to be sure, but not one to attract the attentions of the literati.

There was no interest on their part in any such thing as "popular culture" in the 1920s. The study of folk music and jazz was regarded as an eccentricity by professional musicologists; anthropology was only beginning to emerge as a reputable discipline in our universities; and even the most respectable American literature appeared to be of little interest in college English departments.

Librarians had little use for popular fiction. In 1928, the American Library Association warned that "many of the staid old conservative magazines of the past are now distributors of social and political theories of at least doubtful desirability, and of fiction of whose desirability there is, unfortunately, little or no doubt."

Book reviewers had little to say about science fiction; but then, there weren't really any science fiction books to review. Novels embracing scientific or pseudo-scientific themes were occasionally published, but neither book publishers nor book reviewers thought to use the term "science fiction" until World War II. For its first two decades, the market for modern science fiction (by which I mean science fiction written by people who *knew* that they were writing something called "science fiction") was almost entirely a magazine market. Very few of the writers who wrote for the science fiction magazines were able to interest commercial book publishers in their work. And there weren't too many regular readers of "literary" novels and story collections who frequented the pulp-magazine racks at their corner newsstand.

So, science fiction kept a low profile in those first twenty years. A couple of intrepid explorers from the *North American Review* and *Harper's Magazine* ventured into the pulp jungles and returned with mild praise for science fiction, if only in comparison with other pulp genres. But it's accurate to say that the years from 1926 to 1945 were, for the science fiction field, a period of incubation, in which SF writers developed the literary techniques and conventions of their genre in almost undisturbed isolation from the world outside.

And then, on an August day in 1945, the world learned, in the most shocking way imaginable, of the existence of the atomic bomb. *Astounding Science-Fiction's* editor, John W. Campbell, remembered that "During the weeks immediately following that first atomic bomb, the science-fictioneers were suddenly recognized as not quite such wild-eyed dreamers as they had been thought, and in many soul-satisfying cases became the neighborhood experts."

Campbell wasn't the only editor who considered science fiction writers uniquely qualified to explore the new world that the atom bomb brought into being. *Harper's*, *Collier's*, and the *Saturday Evening Post* published stories by such writers as Miriam Allen DeFord, Robert Heinlein, Ray Bradbury, and Will Jenkins. These were tame stories by the standards of the science fiction magazines: set on the Earth, the Moon, or Mars, in the relatively near future of the 20th and 21st centuries, with no non-human characters. They were presented to readers simply as stories; the words "science fiction" nowhere appeared. And they received an enthusiastic reception.

Serious examinations of science fiction began to appear in a wide range of magazines. At first, these focused on the science fiction community, and were concerned with what sort of people read, and wrote, science fiction. The influential *Saturday Review of Literature* published several articles on science fiction during those postwar years; their common theme was that science fiction was a literature of real importance, preparing readers to discover and accept the realities of the future.

In the early 1950s, science fiction attained a level of popularity and public consciousness not to be duplicated for another twenty-five years. The number of science fiction magazines reached an all-time high; more publishers than ever before were issuing SF books in hardcover; and a new phenomenon, the science fiction paperback, was crowding the newsstands. In the cinemas and on radio, primitive dramatizations of science fiction attracted new audiences to the genre. And the newest medium of all was itself a science-fictional device not many years before. Television was America's latest novelty, and anything about it fascinated the American public.

There were several science fiction programs on television, most of them intended for children. And there were many articles about these programs in American magazines, such as *Newsweek, Time, Life,* and the *New York Times Magazine.* While these articles may have drawn more attention to science fiction, they offered little substantial content. But in a wide range of more intellectually-oriented magazines, science fiction was beginning to undergo an unprecedented level of scrutiny.

Those who concerned themselves with science fiction's literary qualities were usually disappointed by what they found. Characterization was inadequate, plots childish, and authors' imaginations "undisciplined." (Whatever gave Arthur Koestler the idea that a *disciplined* imagination would be an asset to a science fiction writer?) But the *literary* qualities of science fiction were of comparatively little importance in the days of Senator McCarthy.

During those years, the popular arts in America were the subject of investigations—both official and unofficial—into their political significance. The red-hunters didn't concern themselves with science fiction; but somehow the field got a reputation as a haven for ideas which might get their perpetrators into trouble if expressed in other forums.

The veteran SF writer and editor Frederik Pohl likes to claim that "SF provided the only really free press in this country" during the McCarthy years. This may be an exaggeration; but there were a lot of people who found in the science fiction field a lively forum for social criticism, in a period when more popular media were avoiding controversial subject-matter. The intellectual freedom of science fiction excused, for many critics, its literary deficiencies.

Not that science fiction got off unscathed. The genre came under severe attack from psychologically and theologically oriented critics, who considered it a dangerous substitute for religion, and an incitement to neglect mundane problems. Roman Catholic writers tended to judge science fiction in terms of its conformity or opposition to Catholic doctrine, rather than on its own terms. One writer in the Jesuit weekly, *America,* warned that "In the wrong hands [science fiction] can and will create new heresies and revive old ones. In the right hands it can be one more instrument to glorify God." But the important thing here is not the warning against science fiction's potential for heresy. When a Catholic theologian talks of science fiction as an instrument for the glorification of God, the genre has come a long way toward respectability.

Toward the end of the 1950s, interest in science fiction waned. The national fascination with ideology had dissipated, and the boom in science fiction publishing, which had seen as many as thirty-eight SF magazines in existence at one time, had come to an end. By the time the Russians launched Sputnik in 1957, science fiction's value as a guide to the future was dismissed by many outsiders; as Anthony Boucher lamented, "science fiction is looked upon as no longer wildly imaginative but as prosaically passé." Not that mainstream critics ignored the genre: but their articles tended to take a narrow view of the field, emphasizing its visions of their own specialties: architecture, communication, computers, religion, sociology, engineering.

In the more literary magazines, there were extended considerations of the "literary sensibility" of science fiction. Some of these articles were pretty silly. Michel Butor suggested in the *Partisan Review* that the weakness of modern science fiction lay in its failure to present a coherent view of the future. He called on science fiction to "limit and unify itself," by using as a common setting for all SF stories "a single city, named and situated with some precision in space and future time." As James Blish hastened to point out, this prescription "would destroy everyone's interest in either writing or reading it." (But Blish later went on to write several *Star Trek* novels. Perhaps Butor got the better of the argument, after all.)

In the wake of Sputnik, though, there arose a generation of Americans for whom science fiction had been a regular part of youthful reading. During the 1960s, the major American literary publications carried many articles about modern science fiction. This wasn't the literary slumming that had characterized mainstream writing on SF for its first twenty years, nor was it the naive exploration offered by the mainstream journalists and essayists of the '50s. It was rather the product of men and women who had grown up with science fiction, who had some idea of what it was and what it could be, and who judged it by those standards.

Meanwhile, science fiction was beginning to find its way into the classroom and the library. So long as science fiction remained a creature of the pulp magazines, teachers and librarians displayed hostility, or at least indifference, to it. It wasn't until SF books began to appear in hard covers from trade publishers—a process that began in 1946— that science fiction began to earn the cautious approval of librarians and educators.

Through the '50s and '60s, innovative teachers began to use science fiction in their classes, and SF was routinely represented in high school literature textbooks— typically by a rather tame Ray Bradbury story. Quite a few articles appeared in the professional journals—there were more than thirty during those two decades—the great majority of them positive about SF's popularity among young people and its value as illustrative material, to supplement classroom study in the biological, physical, and social sciences.

By the end of the '60s, modern American science fiction was a minor, but accepted, part of the American high school curriculum, and was often used in lower grades as well. This situation continues today, though the presence of science fiction in the curriculum has come under attack from religious fundamentalists and educational conservatives demanding a return to the basics.

In colleges, too, science fiction found a place. Though Sam Moskowitz taught a course in science fiction writing at New York's City College as early as 1953, it was not until 1962 that a formal course in science fiction received the approval of a university English department. Mark Hillegas, who taught that course, was disheartened by the opposition of many of his colleagues. In 1967, he announced that there was "little point at this time in a regular course in science fiction," because of the intellectual conservatism, and the hatred for science and technology, characteristic of English professors.

Like many science fiction prophets, Hillegas turned out to be wrong: by 1971, only four years later, there were at least 200 courses in science fiction at colleges and universities across North America. Today there are courses in the history of science fiction, the literary theory of science fiction, the writing of science fiction—and even the teaching of science fiction.

Some of this can be attributed to science fiction's popularity among college students—English departments live by the ratings, too. The acceptance of such new academic pursuits as women's studies and ethnic studies made it easier for science fiction to find a place on campus. And there was a population explosion in the university, as all of those graduate students churned out on the academic assembly lines of the '60s began their careers.

For many young instructors and assistant professors in pursuit of tenure, science fiction scholarship was the obvious thing to publish. Some observers worried that the field would attract academic opportunists; and Dena Benatan's slogan, "Let's take science fiction out of the classroom and put it back in the gutter where it belongs," became a popular rallying-cry. But many of these young science fiction scholars were SF fans, who seized the opportunity to combine business with pleasure. Before long articles on science fiction were appearing in a wide range of journals from a wide range of disciplines, and a flood of book-length studies began to issue from university presses and other scholarly publishers. Much of this activity took place in emerging journals, or at second-rate universities trying to make a name for themselves: but many of the most prestigious institutions in American academic life were represented, too.

Where there are books, there are librarians; and research libraries began to collect science fiction. Syracuse University's pioneering collection of SF manuscripts was started in 1965; today there are at least two dozen American libraries with substantial research collections. Several publishers issued microfilm editions of science fiction magazines and reprint editions of out-of-print SF classics, allowing many other libraries to assemble representative collections of American science fiction.

Science fiction was also gaining a foothold in the public library. Pulp magazines repelled librarians, but the changeover to digest size that began during the 1940s had brought some titles to library shelves. It was the availability of hardcover books from respectable publishers that really opened the libraries to SF. Beginning in 1946, several anthologies collected the best stories from the Golden Age of *Astounding* and its rivals. The so-called "juvenile" novels of Robert Heinlein and Andre Norton—who was a children's librarian herself—rapidly gained the approval of young-adult librarians in school and public libraries. The consequences of this were of great importance to science fiction: for the "juvenile" market was a lucrative one—after all, a new audience comes along every few years, and the same book can be sold over and over to each successive crop of twelve-year-olds—and for the first time it became possible for someone to write science fiction full time without starving to death, and without having to grub out hackwork at a penny a word for the pulps.

Thus modern science fiction gained an unprecedented visibility on the American literary scene. But perhaps the most exciting aspect of science fiction's "descent into respectability"—to borrow Paul Carter's marvelous phrase—is its role as an aid to futurological research.

Futurology is one of many possible names for the scientific study of the future, what Dennis Livingston has described as "the art-that-wants-to-be-a-science of forecasting or anticipating alternative futures from which we may choose desirable directions for society's development." The relationship between futurology and science fiction has been an ambiguous one. Starting with H. G. Wells, there have been many people active in both fields. But futurology has never achieved such respectability itself that it can freely associate itself with science fiction, and there have always been those who have used "science fiction" as a pejorative for concepts to which they cannot subscribe. For example, a midwestern psychologist refused to attend a symposium on "Man in Space" at an American Psychological Association conference, explaining that "he had not come all the way from Minnesota to listen to science fiction"—this on the eve of Sputnik!

But there have been more imaginative people in the field. The late Herman Kahn wrote a short SF story (he called it a "fictionalized scenario") to illustrate a point in his book *The Year 2000*. And the inventors of the Delphi technique, Olaf Helmer and Theodore Gordon of the Rand Corporation, included Isaac Asimov and Arthur C. Clarke among the panelists on whom they first tried it out.

One of my favorite examples of the use of science fiction in futurological research occurs in a massive volume on *Law and Public Order in Space*, published back in 1963 by the Yale University Press. Fifty pages of that 1100-page work are devoted to "Potential Interactions with Advanced Forms of Non-Earth Life." There being no case law on relations between humans and extraterrestrials, the authors refer to studies in anthropology and in colonial history—and to science fiction stories by the likes of C. S. Lewis and Walter Miller Jr.

It's not only science fiction *stories* that are used by students of the future. In the last twenty years, several leading SF writers have become prominent as consulting futurologists. Isaac Asimov, Arthur C. Clarke, Frederik Pohl, Frank Herbert, Poul Anderson, and Jerry Pournelle have spoken on the lecture circuit and served as resource people in future-oriented projects. One writer told me that most of his corporate employers "prefer not to be mentioned publicly; they don't want to be accused of frivolity by the shareholders, which tells you we've come a long way but we're not there yet." That may be true: but when a corporation pays a hefty consulting fee to an SF writer, then there's somebody in its upper echelon who has a high regard for science fiction.

How did science fiction become respectable? Well, how did it become disrespectable in the first place? Was it because it was crudely written—you don't do too much rewriting at a penny or less a word—and crudely printed?

Or was it because science fiction heroes were scientists and engineers, rather than bullfighters and businessmen? Adultery has always outranked technology in its appeal to the American reader, whether his favorite reading matter be the *National Enquirer* or the *New York Review of Books*. The world's work, and the men and women who do it, have never been of much interest to many of our illustrious writers and to most of our so-called "literary intellectuals."

Modern science fiction was pretty crude stuff at first: bug-eyed monsters improbably lusting after mad scientists' beautiful daughters; scientific geniuses lecturing each other—often incorrectly—on the principles of elementary physics; new elements discovered without even a polite nod in the direction of the Periodic Table. But it matured. Heinlein taught his fellow-writers how to work the necessary background information into the fabric of the story. Getting to the stars was subordinated to thinking about what men and women would do when they got there. And writers and readers became familiar enough with the themes and techniques of science fiction that they didn't have to reinvent the spaceship with every story.

Some people speak of those years as a period of exile from literature, and tell us that science fiction would be stronger and better today, were it not for those years in the "pulp ghetto." But there's another way of looking at that experience: as a sort of "hothouse," in which science fiction advanced more quickly than ever it would have in the mainstream.

Science fiction spent twenty years in near-total isolation from American intellectual life. But by the end of World War II, it had evolved to the point where it could say something meaningful about so frightening an innovation as the atomic bomb. The outside world began to take science fiction seriously, for SF writers were the only people, outside Los Alamos and Oak Ridge, who gave any indication of knowing what a post-atomic world might be like.

Seizing upon this, the leading science fiction writers expanded their markets, peddling their less dangerous visions to Scribner's and the *Saturday Evening Post*. Book publishers, with twenty years' worth of stories to choose from, gave a good impression of the field with the anthologies they issued. And writers and editors, imbued with a love for their genre unique among the hack-ridden pulps, stimulated an intellectual and artistic growth in science fiction, at the same time that other categories of magazine fiction were disappearing. Just when America needed it the most, science fiction became better reading than ever, and reached a larger audience as well.

Hiroshima, McCarthy, Sputnik, *Silent Spring*, Apollo, OPEC—these names represent some of the changes that have shaped our times. But the greatest force shaping our lives is the certainty of change: the certain knowledge that, whatever the future may bring, it will be far different from the world in which we grew up. Modern science fiction has demonstrated its ability to explore the fact of constant change. Science fiction writers, with their literary roots in the pulp tradition, are uniquely equipped to offer their readers an optimistic view of the human future.

If change is the one constant of our times, hope is the one necessity of our lives. Because science fiction stories are set in the future, they offer the hope that the human race will survive. Because science fiction stories are about human accomplishment, they offer the hope that the human future holds more than mere survival.

Change and Hope, the words that define the human condition in the 20th century, are the themes of modern American science fiction. And it is this—science fiction's increasing relevance to the human condition—that has made modern science fiction an increasingly important part of the American literary scene. By bringing tidings of Change and Hope to its readers in America and throughout the world, science fiction has earned both an unprecedented popularity in the literary marketplace and the respect of a large portion of the American literary community.

Lester and Me

Anyone who reads *Locus*—for that matter, anyone with any consciousness of the history of modern science fiction—knows the basic facts about Lester del Rey's career. Like many of his generation, his education owed more to the pulp marketplace than to the classroom. He was not much impressed by critics and scholars: when he was Guest of Honor at the 1967 Worldcon in New York, his speech was entitled "Art or Artiness," and none of his listeners was in any doubt as to which he favored. But there were few places (if any) where Lester couldn't hold his own, and I was privileged to watch him take on the minions of academe in their own lair.

When I earned my doctorate at the Columbia University School of Library Service, I had to defend my dissertation before a five-person examining committee. School custom ordained that the Committee would include the candidate's advisor and second reader; two members of the SLS faculty whose scholarly interests had some connection with the topic of the candidate's dissertation; and one expert from outside the faculty, chosen for his special knowledge of the dissertation topic. The candidate was invited to suggest outside experts; and he could veto any proposed name. (This minimized the danger of confronting one's academic enemy across the examination-room table.) There was no requirement that the outside expert hold any academic credentials; it was his expertise, not his curriculum vitae, that justified his presence. No one could doubt Lester's expertise on science fiction (or for that matter on anything else; I still have one of his business cards, which reads "Lester del Rey: Expert"); and his history of the field, *The World of Science Fiction, 1926–1976: The History of a Subculture*, covered the same fifty-year period as did my dissertation. My nomination of Lester to serve as outside expert on my examining committee was accepted enthusiastically.

On the morning of my defense, I saw a sight unparalleled in SLS history: several members of a doctoral examining committee were asking another member for his autograph! The examination itself proceeded routinely. With two of the five members having already determined that the dissertation was ready to defend, and with the casting vote that of the candidate's nominee, it would be most unusual for any outcome other than "acceptance with minor revisions." So I settled back for the expected hour or two of nit-picking; and I was not disappointed.

I was easily able to deflect my examiners' questions, save for one. An objection was made to my assertion that during the 1960s, "there have been few, if any, good stories that have not found a market." What was my authority for that statement? I was asked. "Twenty years' participation and observation of the field," I replied; but evidently that wasn't enough. "But he's right," Lester maintained. "May I footnote you on that?" I asked; and one of my "minor revisions" was to attribute that bit of information to "Lester del Rey, interview, 18 March 1981." Compulsive fact-checkers may find that footnote on page 61 of my dissertation. I know that "Modern Science Fiction and Its Reception by the American Literary and Educational Communities, 1926–1970" was a good piece of work. It was approved by Lester del Rey.

11

Towards a Definition of Science Fiction:
A Reply to James Gunn

When I was in high school, I was fascinated with history. Naive lad that I was, I thought of history as simply a straightforward narrative account of what had happened in the past. Four years as a history major in college cured me of that delusion. I learned that an historian's narrative owed something to the events that he described and as much or more to what he meant to do with them.

So it is with the definition of science fiction. There simply is no such thing as *the* definition of science fiction. How one defines it depends on what one intends to do with it. The reader, the writer, the editor, the publisher, the bibliographer, the historian, the teacher, the librarian, the critic—each has his own concerns, and those concerns necessarily shape, not only his working definition of science fiction, but also his entire approach to the question of defining SF.

Let us begin with the reader. He reads science fiction for enjoyment; his concern is to obtain the maximum amount of pleasure for the minimum amount of effort. For him, the working definition of SF is "the kind of stories I like because..."—what follows the "because" is an expression of personal preference that need not concern us. And our quest for a definition of science fiction need not concern him. For he is willing and able to pay for his reading pleasure, and the market will evolve a workable definition to guide him to the cash register.

For the writer who hopes to sell his stories, science fiction is defined quite pragmatically: "the kinds of stories that science fiction editors are buying." The same market forces that serve the reader guide the pen of the writer; and the history of modern science fiction, in America at least, is the working-out of the tension between the writer's imagination and the demands of the marketplace. But to the writer, the market's definition of science fiction is all that matters. It governs what he can sell. No other definition can offer any useful guidance to a writer with his own story to tell.

The editor and the publisher are likewise governed by the market. Each is successful to the extent that the stories he chooses for publication attain a lucrative readership. Market segmentation is as applicable to publishing as to any other form of commerce, so each editor or publisher, in seeking his niche in the literary marketplace, defines his own concept of publishable science fiction. But few editors or publishers would confuse these narrow delimitations with the breadth of science fiction itself—a fact demonstrated by the many instances in our field's history in which a single editor or publisher has produced two or more widely differing lines of SF.

Now, each of the parties I have so far mentioned employs an idiosyncratic definition of science fiction. The reader is answerable to nobody but himself. The writer may present as science fiction anything that his imagination might contrive. And the editor and the publisher may offer as science fiction anything that their readers will buy. As long as the paying customers are satisfied with the bargain, who will argue the matter? *De gustibus non est disputandum.*

But now we come to some actors who must answer to a wider constituency. If the reader adopts an idiosyncratic definition of science fiction, there is no one to judge him. The writer may define as science fiction anything that he can coax from his imagination; and the editor and publisher, anything that they can coax from their writers or anything their writers foist upon them. It is up to them to convince the readers, either through shrewd merchandising or by exploiting the confidence their previous publications have earned for them, to accept these as science fiction. Whether they be called "thought variant" or "new wave," there have been successful attempts at expanding the paying customers' concept of science fiction.

The creators of science fiction (and I include the readers in this category; I'll explain why a bit later) have this freedom, but the commentators don't. The nature of their work requires them to deal with the field as it is. If they pronounce on what science fiction *should* be, nobody will pay them any attention—unless they legitimate their arguments by *writing* the sort of science fiction they want to see. (Does anyone in this room know who Michel Butor is? Is there anyone here who doesn't consider his opinions on SF to be utter nonsense?)

Consider the bibliographer. Now, defining "bibliography" is as tendentious a matter as defining "science fiction," but let's for the moment use the term in its most commonly misunderstood sense: the compiler of lists of books. His work is pointless unless the books he lists conform to some criterion: origin, provenance, subject-matter, physical format, association, whatever. And if his work is to serve any purpose other than the satisfaction of his own vanity, the criterion he employs must be relevant to the interests of others besides himself. Of what use is a Hemingway bibliography whose compiler insists that Ernest Hemingway wrote the plays of Shakespeare? What use could we possibly make of a science fiction bibliography compiled by a man who defined as SF any story set in North Carolina?

The historian is in the same position, for after all he is really writing bibliography in narrative form. (The broader definitions of "bibliography" include literary history within its embrace. I certainly consider my own writing about SF to fall within the category of bibliographical scholarship.) The historian may define to his satisfaction whatever aspect of science fiction he will study; but his definition is one of the criteria against which his book will be judged. He will not, however, have to answer for the correctness of his working definition, but for its utility: does the definition he employs improve or detract from our ability to learn something valuable about SF from his book?

Where the historian attempts to elucidate science fiction's past, the critic tries to illuminate its present. His job is to help us to read more efficiently: to examine the words in a story and the way in which they're put together. As to *how* he should do this—well, there's plenty of disagreement about that, and I've no intention of jumping into that donnybrook. But no matter what his methodology, the critic, like the historian, can communicate his findings only to an audience with whom he shares a common vocabulary.

The teacher and the librarian are still more constrained. Unlike the historian and the critic, they are neither expected nor desired to bring any great degree of individuality to their work. Their value to student or library patron is in direct proportion to the conventionality of their approach. Both must seek to inform their work with consensus rather than originality, for unlike the readers of the historian or the critic their audiences have few if any alternative sources for their services.

Given all these components to the science fiction community—and given the considerable variety within each of these components—it's hardly surprising that we have, not only no consensus as to the definition of science fiction, but not even any consensus as to how we should go about the process.

The dozens of attempts at defining SF that I've seen can, I think, be assigned to three categories, which I call thematic, strategic, and empirical.

A thematic definition of science fiction is based in some way upon the subject-matter of the SF story. Most thematic definitions, like the various definitions that James Gunn has quoted in the first part of his talk, attempt to define SF in terms of its scientific content. Some of these definitions are prescriptive, others ostensive. Alastair Cameron's *Fantasy Classification System*, a thematic decimal classification of fantasy and scientific stories, attempts to include all of the "fantastic properties of the elements which make up a story." This of course makes it a 52-page definition of the genre—but an unsuccessful one: Ursula Le Guin's *The Left Hand of Darkness*, arguably the most important SF novel of the past twenty years, cannot be accounted for under Cameron's scheme.

More recently, "change" has replaced "science" as the touchstone. Gunn has summarized this viewpoint: "Science fiction is the literature of change. Change is its subject matter and its method."

"... And its method." That provides a convenient transition to the second of our categories of definition. The "strategic" approach to defining science fiction focuses not on what the story is about, but on *how* it is written, and read. The pioneers of this approach to science fiction, Darko Suvin and Samuel R. Delany, may intimidate us with phrases like "cognitive estrangement" and "subjunctivity level": but their basic argument, that form and content are essentially identical, offers a fruitful way of looking at science fiction. Closely related to this is the notion that the label "science fiction" is a set of "author's instructions on how to read a work," as Jim Gunn has suggested.

That is why I included the reader among the "creators" of science fiction a few minutes ago. For in following or disregarding, to whatever extent it pleases him, the "instructions" that the author has (consciously or unconsciously) embedded in his story, the reader plays his part in the story's creation, just as the musician plays his part in realizing the composer's intention.

The "empirical" definition comes in many flavors, from Norman Spinrad's "science fiction is anything published as science fiction" to my own favorite definition: "science fiction is the stuff on the brown bookshelves upstairs in my study." When I was studying the changes in modern science fiction's reputation in this country since 1926, it was an empirical definition that I used. I was concerned with how outsiders viewed the field, and their conception of science fiction was necessarily shaped by what was presented to them as science fiction.

My own suspicion is that the search for the perfect definition of science fiction is a futile one. It can be fun, just as choosing the opposing line-ups for an imaginary all-time all-star game between the American League and the National League can be. But, like that activity, it is a pursuit better suited to the saloon than the seminar room, and should really never be approached without a goodly supply of beer within reach.

The attempt to arrive at a perfect definition of science fiction is doomed to failure. Any attempt to define SF, except perhaps for a purely empirical one, pits the ingenuity of the definer against a truly irresistible force, one that we are all gathered here in Atlanta to celebrate: the collective imagination of the world's science fiction writers.

"A Master of Our Art"

"He is for everyone who responds to vividness, word magic, sheer storytelling. Most readers go on to discover the subtleties and profundities. ...Thus his influence pervades modern science fiction and fantasy writing." Thus Poul Anderson, writing in praise of a writer who was born in the 19th century and died in the 20th. He wrote of new inventions and future wars, and warned of the social consequences of technological change. And he exerted an immense influence on modern science fiction.

I'm not speaking of Jules Verne (1828–1905) or H. G. Wells (1866–1946). True, both names come immediately to mind when we seek the roots of science fiction. When Hugo Gernsback founded the first real SF magazine in 1926, he filled out the early issues of *Amazing Stories* with reprints of their stories. The writers who shaped modern science fiction—Heinlein, Asimov, Van Vogt, de Camp—read Verne and Wells as boys. But today their works have achieved the status of classics: much honored but little read. It was their contemporary Rudyard Kipling (1865–1936) who has exerted the most lasting influence on modern science fiction.

Like Verne and Wells, Kipling wrote stories whose subject-matter is explicitly science-fictional. "With the Night Mail: A Story of 2000 A.D." portrays futuristic aviation in a journalistic present tense that recalls Kipling's years as a teenaged subeditor on Anglo-Indian newspapers. "The Eye of Allah" deals with the introduction of advanced technology into a primitive society that may not be ready for it.

But it is not this explicit use of science and technology in some of his stories that makes Kipling so important to modern science fiction. Sam Moskowitz and Bruce Franklin have shown that many of Kipling's contemporaries and predecessors wrote scientific fiction. Nathaniel Hawthorne and Herman Melville, Mark Twain and Conan Doyle are among them; yet echoes of their work are seldom seen in today's science fiction. Kipling's appeal to modern readers lies instead in his approach and his technique.

The real subject matter of Rudyard Kipling's writing, whether in prose or in verse, is the world's work and the people who do it. Whether that work be manual or intellectual, creative or administrative, the performance of his work is the most important thing in a man's life. As Disko Troop says in *Captains Courageous*, "*the* most interesting thing in the world is to find out how the next man gets his vittles."

This is not a view shared by most of 20th-century literature; nor is Kipling's special sympathy with the work of Empire. This explains why Rudyard Kipling has received less attention from the literary community than his writings deserve. But he was an enormously popular writer, especially among working people; and even to this day he is widely quoted, often by people who would be shocked to learn the source of the colorful expressions they so often use. Today's science fiction writers find their audience among the same strata of society that in Victoria's time read Kipling: adults engaged in the shaping of our world, and young people exploring what life has to offer.

Kipling faced the same technical problem that the science fiction writer does: the need to make an alien time and place understandable to his audience. Whether the scene be India under the British Raj or Mars under the Solar Federation, the reader needs to know the essential differences in biology, technology, and sociology that govern the characters and their actions. This information needs to be provided without interfering with the narrative: the reader wants a story, not a lesson.

The legendary editor John Campbell—the man who brought about the Golden Age of science fiction—once explained why he considered Rudyard Kipling the first modern science fiction writer. He was the first to go beyond simply providing the reader with the essential background information needed to read his story. "With the Night Mail" is a pseudo-journalistic account of transatlantic dirigible traffic. In its original magazine appearance in 1905, the text was surrounded with weather advisories, classified advertisements, shipping notices, and a wide range of other snippets intended to suggest that the tale was in fact appearing in a magazine published in 2000. All this stage business was extraneous to the story, strictly speaking; but it did help to establish the setting.

Kipling had learned this trick in India. His original Anglo-Indian readership knew the customs and institutions and landscapes of British India at first hand. But when he began writing for a wider British and American audience, he had to provide his new readers with enough information for them to understand what was going on. In his earliest stories and verse he made liberal use of footnotes, but he evolved more subtle methods as his talent matured. A combination of outright exposition, sparingly used, and contextual clues, generously sprinkled through the narrative, offered the needed background. In *Kim* and other stories of India he uses King James English to indicate that characters are speaking in Hindustani; this is never explained, but it gets the message across subliminally.

Modern science fiction writers and their readers have become so accustomed to this sort of thing—and so dependent on it—that it has made the genre literally unreadable to many who have not learned its reading protocols. Samuel R. Delany has observed that a statement that is meaningless in mimetic fiction (such as "The red sun is high, the blue low") can be a matter of simple description in science fiction, and a statement that could only be metaphorical ("Her world exploded") might be meant as literal fact in SF. It is this divergence in the way words are used, rather than any particular exoticism of subject matter or the use of experimental narrative strategies (here SF is usually very conservative), that separates modern science fiction from the literary mainstream. And all this began with Kipling.

It is certainly a matter of fact that Kipling's works are immensely popular among SF writers. Allusions to Kipling in story titles and quotations from his verse may be found throughout the genre. Autobiographical essays and story introductions widely acknowledge Kipling as a favorite writer and a major inspiration. David Drake and Sandra Miesel have assembled two anthologies of stories written under the influence of Kipling, accompanied by introductions in which the likes of Poul Anderson, L. Sprague de Camp, Joe Haldeman, and Gene Wolfe describe the impact that reading Kipling has had on their own writing.

But the best way to understand why Kipling has exerted so great an influence over modern science fiction is to read his own work. Begin with *Kim*, the most successful evocation of an alien world ever produced in English. Follow the Grand Trunk Road toward the Northwest Frontier, and watch the parade of cultures that young Kimball O'Hara encounters. Place yourself in his position, that of a half-assimilated stranger in a strange land; and observe carefully the uneven effects of an ancient society's encounter with a technologically advanced culture. SF writers have found *Kim* so appealing that several have told their own versions of the story: Robert Heinlein's *Citizen of the Galaxy*, Poul Anderson's *The Game of Empire*, Patricia Wrede's *Mairelon the Magician*.

Then look at *Puck of Pook's Hill* and *Rewards and Fairies*, two collections of linked stories in which Kipling brings incidents of English history and prehistory to life, both for the children for whom the books were ostensibly written and for their elders. One could classify them as time-travel stories, thus bringing them into the taxonomy of science fiction; but their real relevance lies in the careful evocation of time and place echoed in so many later stories which bring a modern observer into direct contact with earlier days.

And by all means read Kipling's own science fiction and fantasy stories. This has been made much easier by the recent publication of two volumes, *Kipling's Science Fiction* and *Kipling's Fantasy*, in which the noted British SF writer John Brunner has brought together pieces from the thirty-six volumes of Kipling's collected works.

Among the nine stories in *Kipling's Science Fiction* are "With the Night Mail" and its sequel "As Easy as A.B.C.," which explore the social as well as the technical side of a world economy based on air traffic. Technological change touches human lives, individually as well as collectively, and in these stories we see that ordinary people as well as heroes will be affected by aerial technology and the social structures set up to govern it. In " 'Wireless'," Kipling captures the excitement of the infant science of radio, and the single-mindedness of the young experimenter. "There's nothing we shan't be able to do in ten years. I want to live—my God, how I want to live, and see it develop!" In parallel with the transmission of Morse across the ether, we share the unconscious communication of a dying lover with the poet who a century before had shared both his emotion and his consumption. "The Eye of Allah" explores a future that might have been, from the perspective of a 13th-century abbey. Kipling manages to re-create convincingly and empathetically the mediaeval attitude toward science and faith. The collection also includes a tall tale about a sea-monster ("A Matter of Fact"), two stories that get inside the soul of great machines ("The Ship That Found Herself" and ".007"), and explorations of the frontiers of psychology ("In the Same Boat") and medicine ("Unprofessional").

The variety of *Kipling's Fantasy* includes children's tales from the *Just-So Stories* ("The Sing-Song of Old Man Kangaroo") and *Rewards and Fairies* ("The Knife and the Naked Chalk"), as well as somber stories like "They" and "The Gardener" that recall the tragedies of Kipling's own life. In "The Finances of the Gods" and "The Bridge-Builders" Kipling works with the material of Indian legend, while "The House Surgeon" is a very English ghost story. "By Word of Mouth" and "The Children of the Zodiac" recall Kipling's brushes with death. But the most interesting stories in this collection are "'The Finest Story in the World'" and "The Village That Voted the Earth Was Flat," two tales that explore that most mysterious of human activities, the act of artistic creation. (If you do not consider a perfectly-crafted hoax the epitome of the creative impulse, you might not like "Village." If you hold the Art of Getting Even in high esteem, you will find it one of the funniest things you have ever read.)

And there's more where they came from. Brunner omits "The Brushwood Boy" and "The Army of a Dream," and no doubt other Kipling enthusiasts will think of additional tales that might have been included. Still, anyone who reads these two books will come away with a good idea of Kipling's astonishing versatility as well as his prodigious capacities as a storyteller. The wide range of his subject matter—his stories are set on every continent, and in every time from the days of the cavemen to the 21st century—together with the contemporary and historical allusions that dot his works can make Kipling rough going for the unprepared reader. Here is where John Brunner's efforts pay off. He knows his Kipling, he knows his English cultural history, and he knows his American audience. In a brief introduction to each story, Brunner explains words and concepts that might puzzle today's American reader.

Rudyard Kipling is a tremendously versatile writer, a superb literary craftsman, and an inspiration to those who have chosen to write of people and the work that they do. Any collection of science fiction and fantasy will inevitably include many stories written under his influence. A good SF collection should also include Kipling's own contributions to the genre. John Brunner has made it easy to do so with these two attractively packaged story collections.

WORKS MENTIONED:

Anderson, Poul. *The Game of Empire*. Baen, 1985.

Delany, Samuel R. *The Jewel-Hinged Jaw*. Dragon Press, 1977.

Drake, David, and Miesel, Sandra (eds.). *Heads to the Storm*. Baen, 1989.

_____. *A Separate Star: A Science Fiction Tribute to Rudyard Kipling*. Baen, 1989.

Franklin, H. Bruce. *Future Perfect: American Science Fiction of the Nineteenth Century*. Oxford University Press, 1966.

Heinlein, Robert A. *Citizen of the Galaxy*. Scribner, 1957.

Moskowitz, Sam. *Science Fiction by Gaslight: A History and Anthology of Science Fiction in the Popular Magazines, 1891–1911*. World, 1968.

Wrede, Patricia C. *Mairelon the Magician*. Tor, 1991.

DISCUSSED IN DETAIL:

Brunner, John (ed.). *Kipling's Science Fiction*. New York: Tor, 1992. xiv, 178 pp., cloth, acid-free paper, $17.95 (ISBN 0-312-85355-6).

_____. *Kipling's Fantasy*. New York: Tor, 1992. xiv, 206 pp., cloth, acid-free paper, $17.95 (ISBN 0-312-85354-8).

Reading About Robert Heinlein

Anyone who wishes to understand modern American science fiction must come to terms with two men. John Campbell defined what science fiction writers were to do, and Robert Heinlein showed how it was to be done. It was Campbell who first provided a dependable market for good science fiction, and Heinlein who broadened the SF market to the point where a conscientious writer could make a decent living from it. And it was Campbell who established commercial science fiction as a forum for ideas—and Heinlein who exploited that forum.

Surprisingly little has been written about Campbell. But a selection of his letters is being prepared for publication; and over the last five years several autobiographical accounts of SF writers have appeared in which Campbell figures heavily. We can expect some major studies of Campbell to appear during the 1980s.

And we are beginning to see some substantial attention paid to Robert Heinlein and his writings. Articles on Heinlein and his work have appeared in several scholarly journals and essay collections; he has been discussed in nearly every book about science fiction; and at least five publications have so far appeared which are devoted entirely to the consideration of his career.

The most substantial books on Heinlein are:

Heinlein in Dimension: A Critical Analysis, by Alexei Panshin (Chicago: Advent, 1980)

SF in Dimension: A Book of Explorations, 2nd ed., by Alexei and Cory Panshin (Chicago: Advent, 1980)

Robert A. Heinlein, edited by Joseph D. Olander and Martin Harry Greenberg (New York: Taplinger, 1978)

The Classic Years of Robert A. Heinlein, by George Edward Slusser (San Bernardino, Calif.: Borgo Press, 1977)

Robert A. Heinlein: Stranger in His Own Land, by George Edward Slusser (San Bernardino, Calif.: Borgo Press, 1977)

Robert A. Heinlein: America as Science Fiction, by H. Bruce Franklin (New York: Oxford University Press, 1980).

The first of these books to appear was Alexei Panshin's *Heinlein in Dimension*. Panshin did not enjoy the cooperation from Heinlein that David Samuelson (in the Taplinger collection) and Bruce Franklin received; Heinlein's response to the book, both during its compilation and after its publication, was a hostile one. Panshin was sufficiently well connected within the intimate confines of American science fiction to receive background information from several of Heinlein's friends and colleagues; but *Heinlein in Dimension* is essentially a critical rather than a biographical study.

More than half of *Heinlein in Dimension* is devoted to a chronological account of Heinlein's career. Panshin divides that career into three periods. "The Period of Influence," between 1938 and 1942, produced a prolific outpouring of extrapolative stories which (according to Panshin) had a substantial effect upon other SF writers. Following a wartime hiatus, "The Period of Success" (1947–1958) saw Heinlein expand both the science fiction market and his own readership, most profoundly through the creation of a new format for science fiction, the "juvenile" novel. It was in this format, says Panshin, that Heinlein reached his qualitative peak. Since 1959, Heinlein's career falls into "The Period of Alienation," in which his craftsmanship has declined as he has become more interested in ideology than in story.

The last third of *Heinlein in Dimension* examines the construction, execution, and content of Heinlein's fiction. Panshin does a good job of showing what Heinlein does, and how he does it. In his stories, Heinlein uses romantic situations which he treats in a realistic manner. He is a master of creating contexts: rather than telling his readers the facts of life on a planet or a spaceship, he *shows* them. And he sets his characters genuine problems to solve.

While Heinlein has created a variety of colorful aliens, "there is one unique and vivid human Heinlein character": a composite which Panshin calls "the Heinlein Individual." He comes in different ages and stages of experience, but he is essentially a competent man, with "three central characteristics: his strength, his singularity, and his ability to teach himself." (The model for the Heinlein Individual, Panshin claims, is Heinlein himself.)

This Individual is the center of the universe, its reason for being. Since "the world exists for him, not he for the world," he must enjoy liberty of action; and he (and in some cases with an elite group of companions) possesses supernormal powers which confirm his competence in all that he attempts. The solipsism that pervades Heinlein's fiction permits his characters to deny death in metaphorical or even literal fashion.

Panshin concludes *Heinlein in Dimension* by suggesting that Heinlein's ultimate reputation will be much like Kipling's—and that, like Kipling, Heinlein will be remembered and read more for his juvenile fiction than for the stories he wrote for adults.

Heinlein in Dimension is written in a rambling, informal style, the loose first person that characterizes fanzine writing. It would have been a better book had the writing been tighter. But it was the first published full-length study of Heinlein, and its impact on subsequent studies has been substantial.

If *Heinlein in Dimension* represents Alexei Panshin's period of influence as a Heinlein critic, then the essays on Heinlein in *SF in Dimension* represent Panshin's period of alienation from his subject. Although both editions (1976 and 1980) of *SF in Dimension* appear under the names of Alexei and Cory Panshin, there is a substantial continuity of viewpoint with *Heinlein in Dimension*. Two major pieces on Heinlein appear in the first edition: "Reading Heinlein Subjectively" and "Time Enough for Love." The second edition adds an eighty-page essay, "The Death of Science Fiction: A Dream." In addition to the sections on Heinlein, there are several essays on other aspects of science fiction, which we will not discuss here.

In "Reading Heinlein Subjectively," the Panshins maintain that an "objective" reading of Heinlein's stories is impossible, because of the contradictions that abound in them. No consistent ideology can encompass them, and no consistent reality is presented in them. A "subjective" reading is the key to understanding Heinlein's fiction. Several of his stories represent crises in Heinlein's personal life; and in many of his stories the subjective reader will see an attempt at resolving conflict among the Self, the Other, and the Demonic.

I didn't find much of this convincing. My own political tastes run to libertarianism, and I can find nothing in Heinlein's science fiction which is incompatible with a libertarian ideology based upon an ideal of absolute personal freedom and absolute personal responsibility. Practical politics, of course, is an exercise in the adaptation of an ideal to real-world conditions, and Heinlein has offered in his stories several possible realizations of the libertarian ideal. I suspect that those who find the political ideas expressed in Heinlein's fiction inconsistent or incomprehensible don't know as much as they should about libertarian theory.

The Panshins are on somewhat firmer ground when they question the consistency of Heinlein's reality. Much of Heinlein's fiction, even that published explicitly as "science fiction," is more fantasy than straight SF. Many of his characters are superhuman, which reduces their utility as exemplars: how applicable are the experiences of a Lazarus Long to us ephemerals?

The Panshins' essay "Time Enough for Love" was written before Heinlein's novel of that name was published. This does not pose as much of a problem as one might expect, as it isn't until the fifty-ninth page (of a sixty-nine-page essay) that the Panshins get around to talking about *Time Enough for Love*. Their principal point is that the question of survival pervades Heinlein's fiction—survival of adolescence in the juvenile novels, and survival of death in much of his adult fiction. Heinlein's solution to the survival of the ego takes the form of a mystical pantheism, though he is reluctant to embrace it.

Alexei and Cory Panshin are too ready to base their comments on Heinlein's fiction upon their unsupported speculation about his personal life. How do *they* know that Robert Heinlein became a science fiction writer in 1939 because "he wanted to know why Robert Heinlein existed"? In both his personal life and his fiction, "time and again, survival is the answer he has settled for in lieu of a larger answer to the meaning of life." One might be able to speak with some assurance of the motivations of an Isaac Asimov or a Harlan Ellison; but Robert Heinlein is a reticent man, and the evidence just isn't on the record.

"The Number of the Beast—", Heinlein's most recently published novel, was an embarrassment to most Heinlein fans—an ungainly, long-winded argument for four voices and continuum craft which concludes with a self-indulgent assembly of the author's friends and enemies, from our own world and from those which his imagination has created. In "The Death of Science Fiction: A Dream," the Panshins reply in kind: their essay is sprawling and verbose, and ends in a conceit as embarrassingly silly as its original.

For those who, like me, somehow missed reading the obituary notice in *Locus*, it will come as some surprise to learn that science fiction is dead. Who killed science fiction? Earl Kemp once conducted and published polls on the subject, but he needn't have bothered. Robert Heinlein killed modern science fiction, and *"The Number of the Beast—"* was the murder weapon.

How's that again? It's really very simple, explain the Panshins. Heinlein's Future History stories are "the spinal cord of modern science fiction." But in *"The Number of the Beast—"* we are shown that the continuum of the Future History is *not* our continuum, and, therefore, the Future History is not the history of our future. Since the Future History is "the backbone, the life-line of modern science fiction," it's clear that Heinlein has deliberately set out to destroy modern science fiction—and that his mission has been successful.

Two arguments against this notion immediately present themselves. In our continuum, history has already overtaken much of the Future History. While some of Heinlein's pseudo-predictions weren't far off the mark (go back to the early pages of *Methuselah's Children* and look at those newspaper headlines from "The Crazy Years" of the 1960s), several of his stories were set in a future that never came to pass. Thus it might be opportune to jettison the Future History—if it were necessary to assume that science fiction readers were so small-minded as to render it necessary. Heinlein warned his readers against that sort of thing in his postscript to *Revolt in 2100*, "Concerning Stories Never Written." He denied any attempt at serious prophecy: his stories were "meant to amuse and written to buy groceries." *"The Number of the Beast—"* might not have been very amusing, but it did buy a lot of groceries. And it is just a story, one that need bear no correspondence to the Future History or to our own reality.

The space devoted to this non-issue, and the silliness of the Panshins' writing in general (did a grown man and woman *really* write page 343 of *SF in Dimension?*) distract attention from some interesting points. The Panshins demonstrate that several aspects of *"The Number of the Beast—"* are common intellectual currency in contemporary science fiction. They assert that today's SF novelists are pessimistic about the public future, and concentrate on their characters' survival among the ruins. (They neglect to consider the neo-utopian novels being produced by feminist and libertarian writers.) And they suggest that pattern rather than fact will be the intellectual focus of science fiction during the next two decades, with music (the embodiment of pattern) replacing science (the embodiment of fact) as the genre's central motif.

According to Alexei and Cory Panshin, "the frame of reference of SF has been decisively and permanently altered by *'The Number of the Beast—'.*" Just as Olaf Stapledon's *Star Maker* was the ultimate Victorian SF book, so *"The Number of the Beast—"* is the ultimate "modern science fiction" novel, and the SF to come will necessarily take it as a jumping-off point. Heinlein's novel "delimits the meta-universe of consciousness that will be the ground of the New Head SF-to-come."

I wouldn't bet on it.

The "Writers of the 21st Century" series, edited by Joseph D. Olander and Martin Harry Greenberg and published by Taplinger, consists of collections of critical essays on leading science fiction writers. Most of these essays are written by academics, and in several volumes of this series the overall impression a reader receives is one of misplaced ingenuity based upon unwarranted assumptions, and interminable speculation on points which could have been resolved by a telephone call to the writer under discussion. The Heinlein volume is better than some others in the series, perhaps because Heinlein is a more complex science fiction writer than Isaac Asimov or Arthur C. Clarke.

I couldn't detect any common thread running through the nine essays contained in *Robert A. Heinlein*; but there are several points which arise repeatedly.

Heinlein's portrayal of superhuman figures, especially in the novels of the past two decades, inspires several suggested explanations. Alice Carol Gaar ("The Human as Machine Analog: The Big Daddy of Interchangeable Parts in the Fiction of Robert A. Heinlein") suggests that Lazarus Long and other characters drawn larger than life represent Heinlein's reaction to man's insignificance in the universe; while David Samuelson ("Frontiers of the Future: Heinlein's Future History Series") sees Heinlein's retreat into personal dreamworlds such as immortality as his reaction to our society's retreat from the ideal of scientific, technological, and societal progress. Robert Plank ("Omnipotent Cannibals in *Stranger in a Strange Land*") regards *Stranger* as a childish fantasy of wish-fulfillment rather than a serious satirical novel; and Ronald Sarti ("Variations on a Theme: Human Sexuality in the Work of Robert A. Heinlein") accuses Heinlein of stacking the deck: his characters' experiences cannot be identified with those of real people.

The social systems portrayed in Heinlein's stories are also discussed extensively. Jack Williamson ("Youth Against Space: Heinlein's Juveniles Revisited") notes that Heinlein "often seems unhappy with the sacrifice of personal freedom that a technological culture seems to require," and cites several portrayals in the juvenile novels of the conflict between individualism and the need for cooperation and social training. Philip E. Smith II ("The Evolution of Politics and the Politics of Evolution: Social Darwinism in Heinlein's Fiction") observes that since *Starship Troopers*, which presented "a utopian social system for all humanity," Heinlein's attention has focused on smaller and smaller groups. And Russell Letson ("The Returns of Lazarus Long") finds in *Time Enough for Love* the linking of individual, family, society, and species, surviving through the instrument of love.

The contributors to this collection raise several interesting minor points. David Samuelson points out that "We Also Walk Dogs—" doesn't really belong to the Future History; and he sees in *Farnham's Freehold* Heinlein's satire on the spoiled American way of life. Ivor Rogers ("Robert Heinlein: Folklorist of Outer Space") offers an argument for *Caleb Catlum's America* (a 1936 novel by Vincent McHugh) as a model for *Time Enough for Love*. And Ronald Sarti suggests that Heinlein frequently uses adolescent and pre-adolescent female characters because they are not yet conditioned into subservience to males.

There are some notable errors of judgment in this book. Frank H. Tucker ("Major Political and Social Elements in Heinlein's Fiction") seems to think that Kettle Belly Baldwin in "Gulf" is a "villain." He is also too willing to infer Heinlein's own opinions from the statements of his characters. This mistake is also made by Alice Gaar, who assumes (in discussing "The Devil Makes the Law," aka "Magic, Inc.") that the Universe as portrayed in an *Unknown* fantasy might be a valid reflection of its author's beliefs!

But in general, Taplinger's volume on Heinlein is a well-balanced collection of provocative and, in most cases, well-informed essays.

George Edgar Slusser doesn't accept Alexei Panshin's division of Heinlein's career into three periods. The forms employed by Heinlein were unrelated to his purpose as a storyteller; they were dictated by the exigencies of commercial fiction publishing. Slusser doesn't see any major changes in emphasis from Heinlein's early years to the present. The basic argument of his two sixty-page pamphlets (*Robert A. Heinlein: Stranger in His Own Land* and *The Classic Years of Robert A. Heinlein*) is that Heinlein is really a literary Calvinist, in whose fiction a small Elect is predestined to triumph over all obstacles. His stories are allegories, materialistic parables. Thus "Gulf" is not a tale of action and intrigue, but rather "an anatomy of election." And salvation, in *Stranger in a Strange Land*, is reserved for those who bear the "inner light"—the ability to grok.

Slusser makes a strong case, and provides an abundance of examples throughout both studies. I wish that he had gone a step further. As a libertarian, I am tempted to draw a sort of ideological sustenance from Heinlein's stories. But ever since reading

The Moon Is a Harsh Mistress I've been worried by doubts as to the relevance of Heinlein's fiction to political and social issues. For the Lunar revolution chronicled in that novel has an outstanding flaw: it depends for its success upon the cooperation of an omniscient, omnipotent computer—a *machina ex deus*, if I may be forgiven some bad Latin. The Martian superpowers in *Stranger*, the immortality of Lazarus Long, and the fortuitous combination of wild talents possessed by the four protagonists of *"The Number of the Beast—"* are all properties which lie beyond the reach—even the generously extrapolated reach—of the people who will be living in future societies. In other words, Heinlein isn't writing about human beings—and that means that the ideologies exemplified in his fiction of the last twenty years are of uncertain relevance to us. We cannot point to a Heinlein-imagined society and say, "we could build such a future for ourselves"; and this damages Heinlein's value as libertarian inspiration. Now, Heinlein has never claimed that as his purpose; and the avowedly libertarian science fiction writers of the last few years have avoided such supernaturalism. Slusser's essays form a useful prolegomena to an assessment of the ideological implications of Heinlein's fictions; should he ever expand them into a full-length book, I hope that he will undertake such an assessment.

The most recent of the books on Heinlein is the only really satisfactory one. Before reading *Robert A. Heinlein: America as Science Fiction*, I would have considered H. Bruce Franklin an unfortunate choice; a radical Marxist seemed hardly the proper critic to discuss a libertarian writer who has often been called a conservative, a reactionary, and even a fascist by those to his political left. But Franklin is eminently fair to Heinlein throughout his book, and though there are places where what I take to be Marxist language poses a barrier between the author and at least some of his readers, in matters of substance Franklin the Marxist does not stand in the way of Franklin the critic.

Franklin suggests that Robert Heinlein's science fiction embodies the spirit of twentieth-century America—"the contradictions that have been developing in our society ever since the Depression flowed into the Second World War." During his lifetime, Heinlein has experienced the most profound period of technological and social change in human history. He has also experienced what no other generation will ever experience: the awesome realization that, unlike his forebears, he will at the end of his days leave a world radically different from the one he entered at birth. In such a world, science fiction is inevitable; and Heinlein is the most popular, most controversial, and most influential SF writer.

Franklin's discussion of Heinlein's career is organized on a chronological rather than a topical basis; political and social issues are dealt with as they arise in Heinlein's work. Naturally, there are places where I would disagree with Franklin's conclusions. I don't think that the female gender of the Venerians in *Space Cadet* "gives a special psychological twist to this book written for adolescent boys"—it's just another way of emphasizing the alienness of an alien society. And the fact that Larry Smith in *Double Star* had to resort to hypnosis to overcome his xenophobia is not a pessimistic testimony to the indomitable prevalence of that sentiment; remember that the Great Lorenzo underwent that hypnosis voluntarily.

And Franklin's politics occasionally get in the reader's way. The vocabulary of Marxist literary criticism may be appropriate when writing for an audience of the faithful, but there are sure to be many readers who don't consider "bourgeois" a meaningful condemnation, and who are not the least bit put off by "a thoroughly non-dialectical definition of freedom." And his distaste for the capitalistic corporation prevents Franklin from noting the contradictory portrayal of such enterprises in "The Man Who Sold the Moon" and *Red Planet.*

Yet the language barrier and the political myopia are occasional flaws, not persistent problems, in this book. It is in such an area as the touchy question of racism that the opportunity for politically motivated distortion, conscious or unconscious, is most likely to arise; and here Franklin acquits himself well. He points out that anti-black sentiment is absent from Heinlein's fiction, save for *Farnham's Freehold,* which he sees as a vision "apparently generated by very specific events in the 1960s." In the 1940s and 1950s a "characteristic anti-Asian racism" exists in many of Heinlein's stories. Franklin doesn't speculate on the reasons for anti-Asian rather than anti-black feelings in a man born in rural Missouri and educated in Jim Crow Kansas City; and he fails to realize explicitly (though he does imply) that Heinlein's anti-Asian sentiments are directed at totalitarian cultures rather than individuals of Asian ancestry.

Similarly, Franklin sees a contradiction between Heinlein's juvenile novels, in which he "consistently attacks xenophobia and dramatizes respect—even love—for the kinds of beings we may find in space," and the "fear, loathing, rage, and hate" directed at the parasitic slugs of *The Puppet Masters.* But here he misses the essential difference—respect for *thinking* individuals regardless of species.

As these comments illustrate, my disagreements with Franklin are minor ones. In a review of *Robert A. Heinlein: America as Science Fiction,* I concluded that this book is "eminently readable, occasionally tendentious, and well documented." Despite the disagreements I have with some of Franklin's assumptions, vocabulary, and conclusions, I'll stand by what I said then: "It is the best critical study of a single science fiction writer that I have seen."

Anyone who undertakes criticism of a living writer runs a risk: his subject may produce books which render previous commentary ridiculous. I've just heard a rumor that Heinlein has completed a new novel. I hope that any revenge he may be tempted to take upon his critics will be expressed more subtly in it than in *"The Number of the Beast—".* I shall be watching with especial interest the reviews and critical essays the new novel generates. For despite their weaknesses, Heinlein's critics offer many provocative approaches to the work of science fiction's most influential (and most frustrating) writer. Despite my disappointment with much of his recent fiction, rereading Heinlein is still one of my favorite literary pleasures: and now that I've read what the critics have to say, I'll have a new excuse to re-read my favorite science fiction writer's stories.

What I Did on My Vacation

In 1953, Robert and Virginia Heinlein set off from their home in Colorado Springs on a trip around the world. Juvenile novels from Scribner's generated a royalty stream more lucrative than the word rates of the science fiction pulps, and Heinlein's talent for marketing had led him to the well-paying slick magazines such as the *Saturday Evening Post*. The money was there, and perhaps there was another motive as well. The consummate professional writer that Heinlein considered himself to be might do well to write and sell a travel narrative.

Today a trip around the world is usually done by airliner or cruise ship. Those options were open to the Heinleins, and the costs would have been similar. A round-the-world cruise on American President Lines was their first choice. But it was the first choice of too many other travelers; no bookings were available. The long hours of over-water flying required in that pre-jet era repelled Mrs. Heinlein. Fortunately, a third option existed: both scheduled and unscheduled shipping services linked the ports of the world, and like train travel, travel by ship was a perfectly normal way of getting from one place to another.

So the Heinleins took train to New Orleans, sailed on a freighter for Valparaiso, flew across South America to Montevideo, and boarded a liner for Cape Town. After motoring to Kruger National Park, they traveled (again by liner) to Singapore, then to Sydney. A disappointingly short visit to Australia was followed by a flight to Auckland, and then in desperation by the long flight to Honolulu, San Francisco, and finally back to Colorado.

It doesn't sound like a very exciting itinerary, and it wasn't. The wildlife of Kruger Park and political unrest in Jakarta provided the only real excitement of the trip. The rest of it was shipboard life, sightseeing in port, and frustration with sordid hotels, wretched food, and bureaucratic stupidity.

One doesn't learn much about the world and its wonders from *Tramp Royale*. In 1953 customs and currency restrictions still reflected the austerities of World War II. There was still a British Empire, and many of its white inhabitants didn't much like America or Americans. There was little opportunity for an American traveler to meet many of its nonwhite inhabitants, and the Heinleins didn't try much to expand those opportunities. They were more interested in Tristan da Cunha than in Zululand, and the deepest regret Heinlein records over missed opportunities was the *M.S. Ruys's* captain's decision not to risk landing passengers on Tristan. A story on that remote island and its people, illustrated with the author's photographs, might profitably be sold to a slick travel magazine, Heinlein explains; but I can't help wondering if the author of "Universe" and "Common Sense" might not have had another reason for wanting to visit Tristan. A remote, inbred island community well away from the world's trade routes might provide a pretty good analog for the passengers and crew of a generation starship.

One doesn't learn that much about Robert Heinlein, either. *Tramp Royale* was written in the hope that a mainstream publisher might buy it and that Americans

26

planning their own travels might read it. The overlap between this audience and Heinlein's science fiction readers could be expected to be almost nonexistent. Thus there is nothing about science fiction in *Tramp Royale*, and no autobiographical details other than those needed to elaborate the incidents of the voyage. We never even learn Mrs. Heinlein's name: she is called "Ticky" throughout. Though in 1953 Robert Heinlein's imagination had roamed the stars and planets, had journeyed through times past, present, and future, and had explored alien dimensions, the writer of *Tramp Royale* is very much the white-collar American whose days have been spent indoors at a typewriter and whose evenings have been passed in the company of other middle-class midwesterners. His shipmates are no more interesting, nor are the people he meets on his journey. *Tramp Royale* is, alas, the story of a dull American couple who bring their dullness with them around the world.

How much better a travel narrative Heinlein might have written can be seen by looking at the first few pages of *Job: A Comedy of Justice*, one of the more readable of his later novels. And even in the early 1950s, Heinlein was describing in loving detail the exotic landscapes of Mars (*Double Star*) and Venus (*Between Planets*). We can ascribe *Tramp Royale*'s dullness, I think, to the audience to which it was addressed: middle Americans to whom a South American seaport or the Transvaal veldt or the Raffles Hotel in Singapore was the most exotic place to which they could imagine themselves traveling in the flesh.

And that was why *Tramp Royale* languished unsold for forty years. It chronicled the misplanned journey of two Americans whose most notable characteristic was a grumpy dissatisfaction at not encountering the standards of courtesy and comfort to which they felt entitled. It is not a book that would have taught their contemporaries anything useful. And to the better-traveled denizens of the 1990s, it offers even fewer lessons. Robert Heinlein was, in those days and for decades thereafter, a great storyteller. But he was no John Gunther, and no Jan Morris.

If a world creator turned world traveler makes a hash of the task, is the result any better when the situation is reversed? In *Last Letters from Hav*, we have the opportunity to find out.

Hav, a small city-state on the Levantine coast, has been conquered by every passing army since before the Crusades. During the 19th century it was claimed by all the Great Powers of Europe, before being ceded to Russia to provide the czar with an outlet to the Mediterranean. The population of Hav is a layered one: whatever genes were indigenous to the place have been irretrievably mixed with those of all Europe and Asia: Slav and Turk, Greek and Armenian, Arab and Jew. The occupying Powers have left their mark on the city's architecture and its demography: English and French, German and Italian, Austrian and Russian. There's even a Chinese colony by the casino. It's the sort of place where fading aristocrats and remittance men serve as bit players in the game of international intrigue; the slogans might have changed, but the game really hasn't. There's more than a chance resemblance to Durrell's Alexandria.

Jan Morris brings to Hav the same powers of observation that she does to Sydney or Oxford or Manhattan, the same ability to link past and present. The economy and politics of the place are well explained, and one can readily imagine what living there must be like. (Excruciatingly dull, these days!) The only inconsistency in her account comes at the end: as Morris hurriedly departs one step ahead of an invading fleet, one must wonder why any would want the place. But how many of the small wars of our time make much sense to anyone not intimately involved?

The only thing that differentiates *Last Letters from Hav* from other good travel writing—from, say, the sort of thing one might read in the *New Yorker*—is that Hav does not exist. It is wholly the creation of Jan Morris's imagination. Its nearest literary cousin is the utopian novel: a tale in which an imaginary society is the focus of attention, and the narrator merely the lens through which the writer's and readers' attention is focused.

"It's a great place to visit, but I wouldn't want to live there." There is no good reason that utopia must be a perfect country, or even a desirable one. Remember that Thomas More's title was a pun: "utopia" can mean "no place" as well as "good place." From the perspective of the traveler, for whom excitement outweighs comfort and a lively history is of more interest than a settled constitution, Hav offers the perfect combination of the familiar and the exotic. And, just as the science fiction tradition subordinates character to plot and setting, so the ideal travel narrator is a self-effacing one. In *Last Letters from Hav*, Jan Morris transcends this tradition.

In his *Saturday Evening Post* stories, Robert Heinlein won over an audience unused to the concepts of science fiction by focusing on the day-to-day details of human life in an exotic environment. The details that concerned him while on his *Tramp Royale* trip had little to do with the far-away places that he visited. Bureaucracy and discourtesy are all-too-familiar discomforts of daily life at home, and are hardly worth traveling across the world to experience, even vicariously.

To Jan Morris, travel and its incidents are part of the great adventure of life; and, just as an autobiographical anecdote often gains handsomely from a burnishing of the truth, so a traveler's tale is all the richer for taking some economy with the facts. ("Truth is a precious thing, not to be squandered idly on chance-met strangers," as Kimball O'Hara once said; and who would know more of travel or of adventure?) We read travelers' tales in the hope of sharing the traveler's ability to appreciate the infinite variety of the world around us, and we read science fiction for the excitement of imagining worlds beyond. *Last Letters from Hav* captures the adventure of travel, and something of the cosmic adventure of science fiction as well.

BOOKS DISCUSSED

Robert A. Heinlein, *Tramp Royale*. New York: Ace Books, 1992.
Jan Morris, *Last Letters from Hav*. New York: Random House, 1985.

The Posthumous Heinlein

Robert Anson Heinlein died in 1988. For nearly fifty years he had been one of the dominant figures in science fiction, bringing to the field both new techniques of storytelling and new approaches to building a writing career. It was Heinlein who perfected the process of describing a society between the lines of a story, so that by the tale's end the reader felt as though he had lived there all his life. And it was Heinlein who expanded the markets for science fiction stories beyond the pulp magazines, first with sales to *Collier's* and the *Saturday Evening Post*, and then with hard-cover novels packaged for teen-age readers. These new markets not only provided an economic alternative to the low-paying pulps; they also got modern science fiction into bookstores and libraries. There was another, even more profound, influence that Heinlein exerted on American science fiction. For decades new SF writers not only learned their trade by adopting Heinlein's techniques, they absorbed their very conception of what science fiction was from reading his stories. Isaac Asimov or Ray Bradbury might have had a greater impact on the American consciousness; but within the science fiction field itself it would be hard to argue that any other writer did more to shape the genre than did Robert Heinlein.

Certainly my own views of science fiction were shaped by Robert Heinlein. I began reading his novels when I was thirteen, and made a point of finding every story and article that he had ever published. Over the years I read and reread his tales, enjoying not only the excitement of his plots and the environmental and social details of their settings, but also the exaltation of individual liberty and the exuberantly optimistic view of the human prospect that pervaded them. My own feeble essays at writing SF stories show something of Heinlein's influence, though alas nothing of his talent.

Over the years, as my reading in science fiction and in SF criticism deepened, I came to lose some of my regard for Heinlein. His value as a prophet of libertarianism was diminished by the way he stacked the deck: Lazarus Long's immortality and Valentine Michael Smith's Martian superpowers made their actions and opinions irrelevant to the merely human condition. The mysticism that pervades so much of his work calls into question the scientific and technological abilities that Heinlein regularly extolled both in his stories and in his polemical writings. And the solipsistic self-indulgence that characterized the last decade of his writing became very tiresome very quickly.

Still, there is no doubt of Heinlein's historical importance to modern American science fiction; and there are still many readers to whom Robert Heinlein remains one of the field's literary giants. Thus it's not surprising that his novels and story collections are continually reissued. There has also been a steady stream of posthumous publications: of nonfiction unpublished during his lifetime, novels revised to undo editorially imposed changes, previously uncollected minor stories and ephemera. What do these books add to our understanding and appreciation of Robert Heinlein's literary legacy? What need do they fill in a library collection?

Grumbles from the Grave (Ballantine Books, 1990) is a collection of Heinlein's letters, edited by his widow, Virginia Heinlein. Anyone who knew of Heinlein's intense sense of privacy would not have expected this book to reveal much about the man; the "Short Biography of Robert A. Heinlein" with which it begins is only eight pages long, and three of those are occupied by photographs. The letters themselves aren't much more revealing. They are arranged topically, rather than chronologically, and they are chosen to illustrate Heinlein's career as a writer. Many of the letters were written to editors and agents, especially to Lurton R. Blassingame, who represented Heinlein during most of his career. While their presentation in this form makes it easy to trace the progress of individual books, there is very little in *Grumbles* from which one can understand the hopes, fears, and sentiments behind them. Two of Heinlein's enthusiasms—cats and travel—are covered to some extent. But Robert Heinlein is as much a stranger to the reader after *Grumbles from the Grave* as he was before.

Tramp Royale (Ace Books, 1992) is an equally unrevealing book. In 1953, the Heinleins set off from their home in Colorado Springs on a trip around the world. They took train to New Orleans, boarded a freighter for Valparaiso, flew across South America to Montevideo, and sailed from there to Cape Town. While in South Africa they motored to Kruger National Park, then crossed the Indian Ocean by liner to Singapore and Sydney. After a disappointingly short visit to Australia, they flew to Auckland, and from New Zealand flew back home by way of Honolulu and San Francisco. It's not an unconventional itinerary, and by their account the Heinleins weren't unconventional Americans. Perhaps they brought more to their travels than is evident here; I certainly hope that they gained more from the trip than their account would suggest. After reading *Tramp Royale* one would wonder how a man who had created so many fascinating worlds could have found so little of interest on Earth. (Read Rudyard Kipling's *American Notes*, and see how much wonder a young man whose imagination was formed in the bazaars of India could find on the sidewalks of urban America.)

There's a simple, mercenary explanation for the tedium of *Tramp Royale*. Heinlein wrote this narrative in the hope that a mainstream publisher might buy it and that Americans planning their own travels might read it. There would be little overlap between this audience and Heinlein's science fiction readership, and thus no reason to mention science fiction in the book. Furthermore, its hypothetical readers would be interested in the travel experiences of an ordinary middle-class American, not the inner life of so exotic a creature as a professional fiction writer; autobiography would be out of place here. *Tramp Royale* is a book for Middle America: for people to whom Kruger National Park or the Raffles Hotel in Singapore is the epitome of the exotic. But it has nothing to offer young readers in the 1990s.

Many of Heinlein's *Grumbles* are directed at the meddling habits of editors; the science fiction field has seen its share of enthusiastic meddlers. How much damage was done to his stories by editorial interference? Judging from *Stranger in a Strange Land*, less than none.

Thirty years after the publication of the novel that brought Robert Heinlein to national prominence, *Stranger in a Strange Land* was reissued in "the original uncut" version (Ace/Putnam, 1991) with "every word, every turn of phrase, exactly as Heinlein intended it." Sixty thousand words longer than the 1961 edition, it restores "a few scenes that might then have been offensive to public taste."

Is it a better book than the original? Here is how *Stranger* opened in 1961:
"Once upon a time there was a Martian named Valentine Michael Smith."
And here is that same passage, restored to its original glory:
"Once upon a time when the world was young there was a Martian named Smith.
"Valentine Michael Smith was as real as taxes but he was a race of one."
That's enough of a sample to convince me that his editor was right. Heinlein's
later work (everything from "*The Number of the Beast—*" on) would have been im-
proved—rescued might not be too strong a word—if it had been subjected to the
same editorial insistence that pruned sixty thousand words from *Stranger in a Strange
Land*.

I did not re-read the 1961 edition of *Stranger* upon receiving the expanded version; but I cannot say that I noticed anything that materially added to what I remembered of it. To anyone coming to *Stranger* for the first time, I would say this: read the
1961 version, which is not only better written, but is also of significantly more historical importance to the field, and to American popular culture. For the same reasons, libraries that have the original version have no need to acquire the new one.

Another Heinlein novel that an enterprising publisher has restored to its author's
original intention is *Podkayne of Mars* (Baen, 1993), published (as its cover proclaims)
"for the first time with Heinlein's original ending!" When Putnam's first published the
book in 1963, they insisted that young Podkayne Fries survive her captivity at the
hands of the evil Mrs. Grew. In the restored version, Poddy dies. Those seven or eight
pages don't make that much of a difference. In neither version does the story really
end. We never learn the reasons for most of the happenings in the book.

Although *Podkayne of Mars* features an adolescent protagonist/narrator, it doesn't
share the basic feature of the highly successful "juvenile novels" that Heinlein published between 1947 and 1958: a resourceful teenager successfully overcoming major
obstacles in the course of attaining a meaningful goal. Podkayne's Mars, and her experiences on a luxury space liner and on the frontier world of Venus, are showcases for
Heinlein's skills at creating fascinating human societies out of a bit of hardware, a dash
of sociology, and a lavish dose of suggestion. To the reader for whom a new world is its
own reward, the lack of a proper ending doesn't really matter. It apparently didn't to
Heinlein: his point was that "the only basic standard for an adult is the welfare of the
young" (*Grumbles*, p. 87), a theme that resounds through his later novels. Neither the
strengths nor the weaknesses of *Podkayne of Mars* are materially affected by the way it
ends; and anyone who has the older version can find Heinlein's original ending thought-
fully appended to *Grumbles from the Grave*.

*Requiem: New Collected Works by Robert A. Heinlein and Tributes to the Grand
Master* (ed. Yoji Kondo; Tor, 1992) promises "86,000 words of Robert Heinlein—
never in book form before." These include stories from *Boys' Life* and *Calling All Girls*,
guest of honor speeches from science fiction conventions, and material associated
with the film *Destination Moon*. In addition, the book reprints the proceedings of a
Heinlein Retrospective held at the National Air and Space Museum in October 1988,
and fourteen tributes to Heinlein from leading figures in the science fiction field. This
is all material worth reading; but unless one is absolutely dedicated to reading everything that Robert Heinlein ever wrote, or a serious student of Heinlein's influence on
modern science fiction, it is not essential. For most readers, and nearly all libraries, the
price of this book, whether measured in money, shelf space, or reading time, would be

better spent on a novel by one of the many young writers who demonstrate in their own fiction the literary legacy of Robert Heinlein.

Of the five books I've discussed here, only *Grumbles from the Grave* has a real claim on the typical library's limited resources. But Robert Heinlein's place in the library collection does not depend upon a few posthumous publications. I don't think that I am merely expressing nostalgia for my own teenage years when I say that his twelve "juvenile" novels and the "Future History" books assembled from stories he published in the science fiction magazines of the 1940s and '50s are as readable today as when they first appeared. Let today's young readers discover Robert Heinlein through them, and leave his posthumous publications to the devotee and the scholar.

"The Horror! The Horror!"

A few months ago I became the science fiction and fantasy reviewer for the *Wilson Library Bulletin*. I asked that the scope of the "Science Fiction Multiverse" column be redefined to exclude horror fiction. I have no interest in horror, I explained, no sympathy for the genre—and that, of course, would make me unfit to review it. I must not be the only one who feels this way. Certainly my editors at *WLB* were sympathetic to my viewpoint: they readily agreed to drop horror from my purview.

I can't think of any obvious literary reason why horror should be associated with science fiction. In *Supernatural Horror in Literature*, H. P. Lovecraft is careful to distance horror from "naively inspired idealism" and "smirking optimism." Science fiction is inherently an optimistic literature. Its essential subject matter is that most human of activities, problem solving. Its writers have always honored the ideal of applying scientific knowledge and the scientific method to the identification and solution of problems. (There are exceptions to this, of course. *The Genocides* by Thomas Disch is surely science fiction, and it is surely *not* an optimistic story.)

Fantasy writers often choose to ignore science, though there are several fine fantasy stories that instead employ a twisted form of scientific law or technological achievement. (Remember "Magic, Inc." and *The Incompleat Enchanter?*) But in fantasy, too, the prevailing view of the human prospect is an optimistic one. Playing fast and loose with the laws of the universe requires a suspension of disbelief too drastic to be wasted upon a rehearsal of entropy. "Life sucks, and then you die"—we already know *that*. We invest our money, our time, and our dreams in those who can convince us that our lives have some greater meaning.

"The oldest and strongest emotion of mankind is fear," Lovecraft tells us, denying that the human race has advanced in any significant way since we were scared down from the trees. To some of us at least, the strongest human emotion is hope. Where horror fiction is the literary expression of fear, science fiction and fantasy are the literary embodiment of hope; and it is that contradiction which, to me, divorces horror from the SF field.

But how does horror fiction come to be associated with science fiction and fantasy in the first place?

When we speak of the fantasy field, we are really speaking of five categories of fiction that share only one common feature: a significant degree of "cognitive estrangement" from the world we know. It seems to me that these five types of fantasy are characterized and distinguished by the nature of that cognitive estrangement.

In *scientific fantasy*, the cognitive estrangement takes the form of a setting in which the scientific laws and/or technological developments that have shaped our world have taken a noticeably different path, either because of the future evolution of science and technology ("hard science fiction") or because of some assumed divergence from what we know to have happened ("alternate world fiction" or "science fantasy").

33

In *utopian fantasy*, the setting is chosen to illustrate in idealized form the consequences of adopting some socioeconomic, philosophical, or religious ideology. The ideology in question is not necessarily one with which the author sympathizes; its adoption may be shown in a favorable or unfavorable light. (In the latter case "dystopian" is the adjective usually applied to it.)

The setting of *heroic fantasy* is chosen to provide a backdrop against which the protagonist can display qualities that would be implausible in a contemporary setting or in a historical setting recognizable to the intended audience.

Whimsical fantasy uses cognitive estrangement just for the fun of it. We know that animals do not talk, and cannot talk. We do not enquire too closely into the economic infrastructure of the River Bank and the Wild Wood—we just sit back in our easy chair and enjoy the entirely implausible but thoroughly delightful setting that Kenneth Grahame has imagined and shared with us in *The Wind in the Willows*. Whimsical fantasy may be satirical—a tradition that extends back way beyond *Gulliver's Travels*—or written just for the fun of it.

In a *weird fantasy*, the cognitive estrangement also exists to create an atmosphere removed from our daily world. But here the purpose is not to delight but to frighten; in Lovecraft's words, to "[excite] in the reader a profound sense of dread, and of contact with unknown spheres and powers; a subtle attitude of awed listening, as if for the beating of black wings or the scratching of outside shapes and entities on the known universe's utmost rim."

It's entirely possible for a story to partake of more than one of these approaches: *Animal Farm* is both a dystopian (i.e., perverted utopian) fantasy and a whimsical fantasy.

What do these have in common with science fiction? Why are they usually regarded as having something to do with SF? Why am I discussing them here?

There was a time when *Amazing Stories* and *Weird Tales* were the only markets for fantastic fiction, the only place where those who sought the truly unusual in adventure fiction might find it. It was natural for a wide range of stories to find a home in those few magazines devoted to non-realistic fiction. As the science fiction market widened, as the SF readership grew, as the number of writers and editors and collectors and commentators associated with the field increased, they retained the habit of associating horror fiction with science fiction, despite the gulf between their opposing views of the universe.

So why am I so unsympathetic to horror fiction? The easiest way for me to begin to explore this is to look at what I enjoy about the horror fiction that I *do* like.

When I was in college, I traded my small collection of Marvel Comics for a dozen Arkham House books. I've no idea whether this was a good decision from a financial point of view, but I was satisfied then and am satisfied now with the results. I've read the three basic Lovecraft collections, and several volumes of associational material, and I've also read Donald Wandrei's *The Web of Easter Island* and Manly Wade Wellman's *Who Fears the Devil?* What I remember about these books—all of which I read twenty-five years ago and more—is the sense of the exotic that they conveyed. Whether it be a futuristic libertarian utopia, the Harvardian Ruritania of *Islandia*, or for that matter the Regency London of Georgette Heyer's novels, the portrayal of an alien environment in such detail that I can imagine myself fitting comfortably into it is one of the things that makes reading fiction such a pleasure for me. Lovecraft's monsters don't frighten me (most of them are just sashimi on the grand scale); but his protagonists, and the cityscapes and countrysides through which they travel, invite my company.

From what I've seen and heard of it, most contemporary horror fiction appeals to different emotions. It's hardly companionable: there's nobody there with whom I'd like to spend an evening by the fireside drinking a good single malt. (Is there such a thing as a *bad* single malt?) It's not inspirational: the essence of modern horror fiction, as I understand it, is that there are problems that simply are beyond human abilities to solve, and that we are none of us immune from them.

"From what I've seen and heard...," "as I understand it": I trust I've given ample evidence that my aversion to modern horror fiction has been acquired from a safe distance. I am not speaking from any expertise. Nor am I in a hurry to acquire any.

The thing is, I get enough of modern horror in my daily work.

I am a bibliographer by trade. The principal product of my endeavors is the PILOTS database, an index to the worldwide literature on post-traumatic stress disorder and other mental health problems resulting from exposure to traumatic events. I have seen close to seven thousand papers on this subject—I believe that I've seen more of this literature than anyone on this planet—and in those publications I've read about more real horror than anyone needs to experience vicariously. The life-long after-effects of child sexual abuse, the ingenious ways in which Pinochet's military intelligence employed police dogs, the professional education of an Iraqi torturer—after learning of such things, what can King or Koontz offer? (And if I want *real* horror, I've got on my shelves a copy of Geoffrey Lapage's *Animals Parasitic in Man*.)

I cheerfully concede that there are excellent modern horror writers. If so knowledgeable an editor as David Hartwell finds sufficient merit in the heritage of horror to assemble historical anthologies of its classic stories, I must acknowledge the strength of its pedigree. And I must admit that any form of literature that attracts admirers such as those who have contributed to this issue of *Niekas* must have some abiding value.

But not to me. I shall confine my horror reading to the scientific literature that I am paid to index. For pleasure I shall choose from the ample harvest of stories about people who solve the problems of life. Even when their solution is simply to find some way to endure adversity with patience and self-respect, there is a nobility there that I would much rather contemplate.

1994 Revisited

Twenty-four years ago I received a mimeographed booklet in the mail. At first it looked like a fanzine, but closer inspection revealed it to be the first edition of an exercise in futurology. Its first page was actually a memo:

> To: The Reader
> From: Robert Theobald and J. M. Scott
> Subject: *Teg's 1994: An Anticipation of the Near Future*

Robert Theobald is a well-known futurologist, author of books such as *An Alternative Future for America* and *The Challenge of Abundance*, and compiler of an anthology called *Futures Conditional*. So far as I can tell, Jean M. Scott has written no other books.

"This might interest you," was written in blue ink across the top of its first page, followed by an illegible signature. I imagine that I received *Teg's 1994* because I was editor of the *SFRA Newsletter*. One of the priorities of the fledgling Science Fiction Research Association was the bringing together of futurological research and science fiction scholarship, so that both the SF story and the scenario could be used in thinking about the future and in teaching people to think in the future tense. The version that I received was a preliminary one, circulated to encourage comment from readers. The second edition, published in 1972 by Swallow Press of Chicago and reprinted in 1975 by Warner Books, was in fact the first to receive general distribution. (I have never seen it, so I do not know to what extent it differed from the first edition.)

The book begins at Owl Rock, a multihogan in Arizona. Twenty-year-old Integra ("Teg") had been awarded an Orwell Fellowship for synergetic research. "The Orwell Foundation," we are told, "was created ten years ago in 1984, by a group of liberal humanists. It was felt that Orwell's role in warning of possible entropic patterns, particularly in his volume *1984*, and in thus helping us to perceive the need for a more humane terran society, should be honored." Before beginning her year of unlimited travel and research, she has gathered with her eleven fellows for an orientation period. It is during this month-long introduction that Teg is to explore the synergetic potential of the coming year and to learn how to use the most advanced communications resources the planet affords as an aid to her work.

Teg's experience of history is different from ours. After the upheavals of the 1960s, the Planning Party and its ally, the Scientist Synergy, emerged as a political movement dedicated to major change in human organization. As a result of their electoral success, bureaucracies were largely dismantled and decision-making devolved to local communities. The entropy of the 1970s gave way to the synergy of the 1980s, as people became aware that society was breaking down and small teams of people organized to improve the "accurate movement of information."

Her experience of economics is also far removed from ours. In the "abundance regions" of her world—that is, the industrialized nations of Europe, North America, and the Pacific Rim—the production of goods and services is adequate to meet "auto-estimated needs." Thus money is no longer in use, except in a few communities "committed to sensory overload." In the "scarcity regions," where "ecofact production is not yet adequate to meet needs," travelers from the abundance regions use credit cards to obtain the goods and services they need.

This economic system seems unrealistic. The collapse of centrally planned economies has demonstrated the importance of free markets as an essential form of information transfer, but one need not look to socialist societies for proof of this. Anyone who has experienced the combination of hoarding and scarcity that exists in organizations with central supply systems is familiar with this phenomenon. *Teg's 1994* concedes as much when Teg describes some unanticipated confusion at the Honolulu airport:

> The principle that planning always ensures spare capacity in transportation has been so long established that people have become careless about communicating their travel intentions. As intention to travel is underreported needs in transportation capacity are underestimated: just like any other ecofact, required transportation capacity is calculated according to information received about estimated needs with a very small surplus added. The only way that transportation can be available when required is, of course, for information to be passed to the travel center. But so many people are now failing to communicate their intention to travel that transportation capacity is now not always adequate to meet needs.

(I wonder what rush hour is like on the highways of Teg's world.)

Teg tells us that travelers are used to a system where there is always room on board for anyone who has reserved space: "If the number of reservations had exceeded the capacity of the plane a second one would have been available." In such a society, what happens when they run out of aircraft? The demand for transport may not be infinitely elastic, but it offers a reasonable approximation. When there is no need to exchange one's labor for a desired good or service, what restraint is there upon consumption? What is the motivation to produce the goods and services that others wish to consume? These questions are not answered in *Teg's 1994*—while in *our* 1994 they are immensely relevant to the debate in America over the provision and financing of health care.

(Teg also tells us that after all passengers with reservations have boarded, "any people who show invisible college priority suffixes board—facilitators in the invisible college, of course, only use their priority cards when their travel is essential." Well, despite the authors' first-page disclaimer, I guess Teg's world *is* a utopia.)

This "invisible college" is the not-too-clearly-described nomenklatura that runs the synergistic society that is spreading across the world in Teg's 1994. It consists of "those who were interested in and competent to work conceptually," implying self-selection, but there is a mechanism for assigning—and removing—the "high priority suffix to your identity number" that characterizes its members. The existence of those identity numbers, and the requirement that "every member of the invisible college is expected to be available for communication at all times," makes me wonder whether George Orwell would have been entirely pleased to have his name associated with this enterprise.

The greatest weakness of *Teg's 1994*, whether considered as a utopian fiction or as a futurological scenario, is that it concentrates on the activities and thoughts of a narrow segment of the ruling class. We learn that air travel is readily available, apparently at no cost to the user; but we do not learn anything about the lives and motivations of the pilots, the mechanics, the flight attendants, and the toilet scrubbers whose endeavors make air travel possible. It is easy to understand why young Integra would aspire to become part of the invisible college (why does the phrase "The Instrumentality of Mankind" keep popping into my head here?) that runs human affairs. It is less easy to understand why in a money-free society someone would want to pick up the garbage, empty the bedpans, or slaughter the hogs. In the absence of a coercive mechanism—and no system of law enforcement is mentioned anywhere in *Teg's 1994*— how are these unpleasant but necessary jobs done? Members of the invisible college may well proclaim that "conceptual skills ... should receive no more recognition than practical skills," but neither Teg nor those with whom she interacts seems to share that belief.

There's a simple explanation for this. *Teg's 1994* is addressed to those who are interested in "an anticipation of the near future." Such folk tend to be members of the chattering classes rather than people who use their hands on tools more substantial than a keyboard. Like too much utopian literature, like too much science fiction, *Teg's 1994* is concerned with the thoughts and deeds and feelings of highly educated people who manipulate symbols for a living. Rudyard Kipling's interest in the men who performed the real work of the world removed his writing from the modern literary canon; and Allen Steele's depictions of the blue-collar side of living in space place him among a small minority of contemporary science fiction writers.

In revisiting *Teg's 1994* I conclude that the book fails on two counts. Its minor failure is as prophecy: our world little resembles Teg's, and her history has little in common with ours. But that is a minor shortcoming. Nobody in his right mind expects science fiction writers to foretell the future, though they may sometimes be surprisingly right. (Read the news headlines from "the crazy years"—that is, the 1960s— in *Methuselah's Children*, which Heinlein wrote in the early 1940s.) Fred Pohl has a simple explanation for this occasional success: even a broken clock tells accurate time twice a day.

The major failure of *Teg's 1994* is that it purports to describe an entire society while leaving out its most important aspect. We learn how the world is run, and how its dominant thinkers see the evolution of human society. But we see nothing of how this world goes about doing its everyday work, producing the "ecofacts" and "sociofacts" that Teg and her privileged colleagues consume as they flit from continent to continent in the service of Terran synergy.

As a libertarian it pains me to say this, but I would dearly love to see *Teg's 1994* rewritten—by a socialist.

Concerning Purely Personal Preferences

For the past five years, I've been trying in these columns to give *VOYA* readers some idea of the variety and vitality that characterizes modern science fiction and fantasy. I've discussed books, writers, and trends that I think important to an understanding of where science fiction is today and where it is going. But in this final column, I'm going to discuss a few books that have only one thing in common: they are personal favorites of mine. I could excuse this self-indulgence by claiming that it is simply one further demonstration of the range of subject matter and narrative voice that the science fiction literature offers to its readers. But my real motive is simpler. I know of some fine books, and I'd like to share them.

I call myself a science fiction fan, and I have little use for the fantasy-as-yardgoods that clutters bookstores across America. But when I think of the books that have made the greatest impression on me, the books that I pull down from my shelves to re-read or just to savor a few pages, I find myself thinking most often of fantasy stories. Perhaps that's because fantasy gives writers more range for the exercise of imagination than does pure science fiction. The skilled world builder can invent marvelous settings under either set of rules, but fantasy, unconstrained by the need for scientific plausibility, allows more scope for using them.

The Malacia Tapestry by Brian Aldiss is a young man's account of living and loving in a half-European, half-oriental city of immense antiquity. Perian de Chirolo's Malacia is a city at the dawn of the modern age: the internal combustion engine plays no role in its economy, but the passenger-carrying balloon has captured its imagination. It is a city that pays homage to an age-old mythology of descent from dinosaurs—which really exist. Malacia cannot be linked to any place on the Earth we know—yet its citizens quote Aristotle, and fight wars against the Turks. But all that is background. What I find so attractive about Malacia is that its own residents are susceptible to its spell. For all his devotion to the beautiful Armida Hoytola, the true object of Perian's affection is Malacia itself. Nowhere in science fiction or fantasy have I ever encountered a character so evidently a part of his world. And there is no place that I can think of, either on the Earth we inhabit or in any of the worlds I've explored in forty years' reading, that I would rather visit—provided that I could have young Perian as my guide.

Another place I'd like to visit, did it only exist, is Islandia. Situated at the tip of the Karain Continent, somewhere in the general direction of the Antarctic Circle, Islandia has managed to stay out of the world's way for centuries. Foreigners are discouraged, and only a chance Harvard friendship with a young Islandian earned John Lang the opportunity to visit the country, to explore its folkways and its landscape, and to fall in love with the land and its people. In *Islandia*, Austin Tappan Wright has created the most attractive utopia I have ever encountered: and yet managed to sustain the reader's interest through more than nine hundred pages. In most utopian narratives, the traveler from afar who serves as the viewpoint character simply records the differences between his surroundings and the world back home. John Lang, however, is not merely convinced of the merits of Islandian life—after all, that's what a sojourner in utopia is there for—he in fact becomes an Islandian, even though it takes him a while to realize it. Anyone who knows, deep down inside, that there is a better way to spend seven decades on this planet will find confirmation of that knowledge in the pages of *Islandia*.

By contrast, there's nothing at all plausible about the Commonwealth. A land populated by denizens of literature and legend from all the traditions of the world is not a place that any of us would mistake for reality. But if one were a thirty-five-year-old midwesterner of decidedly philistine outlook, one's literary naiveté just might make encounters with Circe, Robin Hood, and Don Quixote seem like the ordinary hazards of being shipwrecked in a strange country. The Commonwealth is no ordinary country, though, and nobody can get through a season there without being irrevocably transformed by the experience. John Myers Myers's *Silverlock* is a tale of transformation, a chronicle of a young man's loss of unearned self-satisfaction and its replacement by a hearty appreciation of the world's possibilities and a confidence in his ability to give them their due. It's also a marvelous literary guessing-game, one that will challenge the reader whose acquaintance with Argentine epic poetry or ancient Irish saga is perhaps a bit incomplete. But most of all *Silverlock* is a celebration of the creative spirit, and the capacity to respond to it.

A vastly different celebration of the creative spirit is *Kaeti & Company* by Keith Roberts. It's easy to fall in love with a high-spirited young woman like Kaeti Fredericks. Certainly Keith Roberts did, when he invented her for a short vampire story. But instead of keeping her in character through a series of sequels, Roberts uses Kaeti and her mates as players in a repertory theater of the mind. Though he places Kaeti in a variety of roles and settings, she retains her essential vivacity. Her adventures (which continue into a second collection, *Kaeti on Tour*) owe more to the ghost story than to scientific or heroic fantasy; but it is the intrepid Cockney sang-froid with which she deals with all that she encounters that wins her creator's heart—and mine.

David Selig is a much less inviting character, an unlovable and unsuccessful young man who ekes out a living ghost-writing term papers for Columbia students. What makes him remarkable is that he is a telepath. His gift has made him neither wealthy nor happy, but it is an essential part of him; and when he begins to lose that gift, the makeshift life that he has fashioned for himself comes apart. In *Dying Inside* Robert Silverberg proves that it is indeed possible to write a gripping science fiction novel whose action is essentially internal. Neither the unhappy Selig nor the decaying New York in which he lives offers anything to gratify the utopian impulse. But there is more to the future than utopia, and *Dying Inside* is one of the strongest examples that I have seen of reducing the cosmic to the human scale.

John Brunner's *The Shockwave Rider* is a much more optimistic novel. It starts off in the dystopian manner, its protagonist subjected to a sinister secret agency's brainwashing. American society is falling apart, despite the efforts of a tyrannical government. Its efforts aren't good enough: technology is a demon that can serve many masters, and the combination of genius and determination allows a small colony of idealists to turn information technology back upon its wielders. In this prototype of the cyberpunk novel, Brunner invented the concept of the computer virus years before computer networks became ubiquitous. More importantly, he portrayed a future in which individual freedom and righteous living remain possible in the face of increasingly pervasive technology. We shall all be spending our future in such a world, and *The Shockwave Rider* shows some ways of making the best of it.

The Star Fox appeared during the Vietnam War, and perhaps Poul Anderson wrote it out of nostalgia for the days in which America's wars commanded popular support and unquestioned nobility of purpose. When the Terran colony-world of New Europe is occupied by the expansionist Alerion empire, the World Federation's response is abandonment and appeasement. But a small brave band, following the demands of conscience in the face of opposition from a craven political establishment, combine ingenuity and courage to defend home, hearth, and honor. It's a common SF theme, but Poul Anderson is to my mind its best player. His heroes are human, and succeed because they possess ordinary human virtues in extraordinary measure. His villains, even the alien Aleriona, are human too, embodying good and evil in varying proportion. *The Star Fox*, like all good science fiction, uses a plausible extrapolation of technology as the basis for its plot. It is the plausibility of its characters and their actions that makes this a great SF novel.

I couldn't write about favorite stories without mentioning Robert Heinlein. The last two decades of his career were marked by an almost solipsistic obsession with tying together all of his previous stories and his philosophical concerns in one huge metafiction, but in even the most self-indulgent of his novels there were substantial passages in which he demonstrated his knack for realizing a plausible new world in a few phrases. Like many others of my generation, I was hooked on science fiction by Heinlein's "juvenile" novels and the stories that made up his Future History. But I would argue that his most successful novel was *Double Star*, the story of an unemployed actor thrust into the role of his life—or rather, of another man's life. Hired to impersonate briefly a leading politician, Lorenzo Smythe's one-night stand turns into a lifetime role. Yes, *Double Star* really is a science-fictional retelling of *The Prisoner of Zenda*, and there is more invention in its politics than in its technology. But what of it? There are only three real plots for a story, Heinlein once said; and *Double Star* is one of the finest examples of "the little tailor" in the genre. Lorenzo Smythe is an ordinary man thrust into extraordinary circumstances, who survives the experience and grows because of it. I like to think that I would do as well, and reading *Double Star* leaves me with the feeling that perhaps I might.

Those are a few of my favorites; I could surely name several more, had we beer enough and time. And there are so many SF and fantasy novels that I've not yet read. How many of them would belong on this list as well? Four decades of reading this literature haven't diminished the wonder and the pleasure that I derive from it. Over the past five years I've tried to share some of this wonder and pleasure with my readers, and with the young readers whom they serve. I hope that I've led a few of them to the excitement and enjoyment that I've found in science fiction. Let me end these columns with an invitation borrowed from e. e. cummings: "listen: there's a hell of a good universe next door; let's go."

BOOKS MENTIONED

Aldiss, Brian W. *The Malacia Tapestry*. Harper and Row, 1977. (Originally published in England in 1976.)

Anderson, Poul. *The Star Fox*. Doubleday, 1965. (Originally serialized in *The Magazine of Fantasy & Science Fiction*.)

Brunner, John. *The Shockwave Rider*. Harper and Row, 1975.

Heinlein, Robert A. *Double Star*. Doubleday, 1957. (Originally serialized in *Astounding Science-Fiction*.)

Myers, John Myers. *Silverlock*. Dutton, 1949.

Roberts, Keith. *Kaeti & Company*. Kerosina Books, 1986.

———. *Kaeti on Tour*. Sirius Book Company, 1992. (Both books contain stories originally published in magazines.)

Silverberg, Robert. *Dying Inside*. Scribner, 1972.

Wright, Austin Tappan. *Islandia*. Rinehart, 1942.

A Librarian Born and Bred

I think that I was born to be a librarian. Perhaps the home movie still exists on which I am captured, at the age of one, removing all the books from a shelf and carefully replacing them—in a different but not random order. Once I learned to read I became one of the Mount Vernon Public Library's most faithful patrons; by the age of ten I was wheeling a laundry cart to the library once a week (twice a week in summer) so that I could transport the ten books that my card allowed me. In high school I was a member of the Library Council, and when I entered college I was fascinated rather than intimidated by the labyrinth that was the Columbia University Library.

I worked part time as a page in Butler Library; I was on duty the night of the great blackout, and roamed through three tiers of stacks encouraging readers to call out so that I could locate them and escort them from the building. Some day I must write down the story of how I became the only employee of the university library system who knew where the Library of Speech Recordings was. Columbia had a penchant for misplacing things. During World War II, so campus legend goes, the library system's main card catalog was microfilmed, and buried beneath South Field for safekeeping. Unfortunately nobody thought to record precisely where it had been buried .... But anybody can lose a few reels of microfilm. A full-size steam locomotive: well, that's another matter.

I might as well tell that story too. The Baldwin Locomotive Works built a locomotive for the World's Columbian Exposition in 1892, and when the fair was over donated the "Columbia" to adorn its namesake's new campus on Morningside Heights. The engine was displayed in the basement of the School of Engineering. Sometime after the First World War, when space grew tight, the "Columbia" was dismantled and crated, for storage somewhere on campus. Nobody has seen it since.

When I entered library school in 1968, I found that my instructors were sympathetic toward my interest in science fiction, and encouraged me to write my term papers on SF. After I graduated I discovered that this hospitality toward science fiction pervaded the library field. My proposal for a paper on librarianship as applied to SF collections was accepted by the Special Libraries Association, and I presented "The Science Fiction Library" as a contributed paper at the SLA's 63rd Annual Conference (Boston, 1972). It was printed in the January 1973 issue of the Association's magazine, *Special Libraries*.

I'm fascinated with library classification schemes, and ever since my junior high school days I've had ambitions to catalog my own books. So it was natural for me to imagine an ideal system for classifying the contents of a science fiction collection. One of my library school projects was the first Conference on the Bibliography of Science Fiction, held at Columbia University in March 1969. (This turned out to be one of the steps leading to the founding of the Science Fiction Research Association.) One of the people I met at the conference was Alastair Cameron, whose *Fantasy Classification System* inspired me to develop my own scheme. When Hal Hall asked me to contribute a chapter to an anthology of essays on science fiction collections in libraries, I revised a paper I'd presented to the Science Fiction Research Association ten years before, and appended to it my Fantasy Collection Classification Scheme. "The Cataloging and Classification of Science Fiction Collections" appeared in the Fall/Winter 1982 issue of *Special Collections*. That issue was also published as *Science-Fiction Collections: Fantasy, Supernatural & Weird Tales* (New York: Haworth Press, 1983).

In 1978, Charlotte Moslander recruited me to review science fiction books for *Voice of Youth Advocates*, a magazine for librarians working with teenagers. Young adult librarians are an unusual audience. Even those who don't care for science fiction recognize a professional need to know something about the genre. *VOYA* reviews were written to help them build good SF collections for their adolescent patrons. A few years later, I undertook to explain to librarians why science fiction was so popular among young readers, and why this popularity was a good thing. "The Popularity of Science Fiction" was published in the October 1982 issue of *VOYA*.

Like most SF fans, my appetite for books outruns both my reading time and my bookshelf space. "Farewell to Alexandria" represents one attempt to find a solution, at least to the second of these shortages. I must admit that I have not yet found the resolve to implement it. "Farewell to Alexandria" appeared in *Lofgeornost* #26 (February 1992).

The Science Fiction Library

Recent years have seen increasing academic interest in science fiction as a literary form. According to a preliminary survey published in May 1971, 61 colleges and universities are offering courses in science fiction; the number is growing rapidly.[1] Many high schools are also teaching science fiction courses. Since 1958, the Modern Language Association of America has sponsored a continuing Seminar on Science Fiction; this annual meeting has been joined by a host of other academic gatherings, ranging from the all-embracing Secondary Universe Conference to special sessions on individual authors or particular research problems. The great interest shown by scholars, teachers, and librarians in the new Science Fiction Research Association is perhaps conclusive proof that the academic world has discovered the genre.

But it is not only the academic who is finding reason to take science fiction seriously. Several professions have found the speculations of SF writers particularly relevant to their own considerations. Religious journals have cited science fictional accounts of other peoples on other worlds in their studies of the theological implications of space travel and contact with nonhuman species. A recent volume on *Law and Public Order in Space*[2] devotes a long chapter to "Potential Interaction with Advanced Forms of Non-Earth Life"; several footnotes refer the reader to SF stories on this theme. Planners in various fields are using science fiction techniques in constructing models of possible future situations.

Neither the academic study nor the professional use of science fiction can be successfully undertaken without access to substantial library resources; but there are few libraries with collections adequate to support research in the field. One of the principal reasons for this lack is the former disregard for science fiction, which dismissed the genre as a form of second-rate pulp literature. As we have seen, this attitude is now obsolete; but there are several other explanations for the inadequacy of library collections in science fiction.

Despite a considerable amount of scholarship and publication by both dedicated amateurs and professional librarians, bibliographical control of science fiction is far from complete. This is only to be expected in a field whose very definition is a matter of extreme controversy. (Indeed, the name "science fiction" is held by many to be a poor choice of word to describe the genre; and such terms as "speculative fiction" and "fantasy" are preferred by several authorities.[3]) A good deal of the bibliographical literature is very difficult to obtain: printed in limited editions, often ignored by library literature and general reviewing media, and distributed by private or semi-professional publishers. Some of the most useful bibliographical information is contained in the catalogs of specialist dealers and in the fanzines—the amateur magazines which have circulated among science fiction fans for forty years. It is probably fair to say that unless one has been active in science fiction fandom for several years, it is impossible to attain a comprehensive knowledge of the bibliography of the genre.

Even when one has familiarized himself with the nature of the field and its bibliography, there are several major obstacles to be overcome before a substantial SF collection can be organized. Until the 1950s, there was little interest on the part of trade publishers in issuing science fiction; so the fans set up their own small publishing houses. "In most cases the editorial choices were wildly capricious; the distributing mechanism was non-existent; the editions were minute; and the profit to author and publisher was invisible."[4]

The paperback revolution had an enormous impact on science fiction. Both reprints and originals flooded the newsstands and bookstalls; a larger proportion of science fiction books is available in paperback than in hard covers today. Many of the most highly acclaimed SF books of recent years are not available in hard-cover editions.

The fact that so many science fiction books were, and still are, published outside of normal trade channels poses a great difficulty in acquisitions. It is difficult to order mass-distribution paperbacks systematically, and next to impossible to obtain those that are out of print. Few bookstores carry the publications of the specialty science fiction houses, and obtaining the address of a specialty publisher is often a difficult matter.

There are, however, bookdealers who specialize in science fiction; many leading private collectors are part-time dealers themselves. They usually handle the books of trade publishers (both American and British), specialty houses, paperback distributors, and amateur publishers; as well as back-issue magazines and second-hand books.

The simplest way to start a specialized SF collection will be to obtain a major private collection in its entirety; this will most likely have to be by purchase, and a five-figure sum will be the going price for such a collection. The days are past when a science fiction collector would gratefully offer his collection to any university that would accept it. Unless there are ties of alumni loyalty, a good science fiction collection will command a high price.

Once such a collection is obtained, it must be cataloged and arranged if it is to be of any use. There are data relevant to the description of science fiction publications which are not provided on Library of Congress catalog cards; and LC printed cards are not available for most SF books anyway. It will be best to plan on detailed original cataloging. If this is done, the publication of the catalog should be considered. In the present state of science fiction bibliography, the published catalog of a really good collection would be a valuable resource.

The use of such conventional classification systems as Dewey and LC is unsatisfactory for a specialized SF library, because not enough detail is provided for in the schedules. With two exceptions, however, no one has developed and published a classification scheme intended for SF collections. Alastair Cameron's *Fantasy Classification System*[5] is intended for classifying stories, rather than books; it cannot serve as a library classification. Any attempt to classify science fiction on the basis of story themes pits the classifier's ingenuity against the collective imagination of SF writers; and it would be only a matter of time before a story was published which would not fit into the classification system. My own Fantasy Collections Classification Scheme has been developed with regard to the peculiar patterns of writing, publishing, and collecting science fiction; while detailed breakdowns are provided for bibliographical, historical, and critical material on science fiction, only form divisions and an optional geographic division are provided for the stories themselves. Plans are being made to experiment with the use of this scheme at a major SF collection.[6]

A more important problem is that of preserving the material in the collection. The curator of Harvard's Clarkson Collection once wrote of "the atrocious pulp on which all the magazines and most of the books were printed," and said that "we cannot allow the material to be handled because of the extreme fragility."[7] It is almost impossible to handle a pre-war pulp magazine without the pages crumbling in one's fingers; and few paperback books can stand the ravages of age and frequent re-reading. Magazine covers and spines and book jackets fade when exposed to strong sunlight.

The more affluent private collectors rely on the usual library procedures—air conditioning, humidity control, absence of direct sunlight, and care in handling—to arrest the deterioration of their holdings. But, for most materials in their collections, this deterioration is inevitable. At the present state of the art, lamination of pages or similar protective measures would be prohibitively expensive. Thus photographic or micrographic reprinting will be necessary to ensure the survival in usable form of much SF material. Because of the scattered nature of manuscript holdings in the field, libraries specializing in science fiction will have to arrange for the exchange of microfilmed manuscripts and other authors' papers. There exists among science fiction collectors and fans a sufficiently large potential market for microform reprints of old magazines and books to provide a strong possibility that well-chosen reprinting projects would be economically feasible.

The librarian who is striving to assemble a comprehensive science fiction collection cannot restrict his attention to the printed word. Such media as pictorial art, film, radio drama, and even grand opera have been used by creators of science fiction. And let us not overlook science fiction and fantasy maps; J. B. Post has assembled a splendid collection at the Free Library of Philadelphia. Slides of magazine covers and book-jacket paintings; prints and stills of SF movies from *Metropolis* to *2001;* tapes of radio and television programs; the score of *Aniara*—all these have their place in the science fiction library. The problems of bibliographical control, acquisition, cataloging and classification, and housing and preservation will be encountered in all these media, of course. The challenges to our professional ingenuity will be fascinating.

The specialized science fiction library is a challenge to build and a challenge to administer. Much of the ground-work has been laid by private collectors; and we librarians will be working with and depending on the collectors in years to come. But it is our responsibility to make collections of science fiction available to the many who would use them, for literary study, for professional speculation, or simply for personal pleasure. Pioneering librarians at Boston University, the MIT Science Fiction Society, and the Toronto Public Library—to cite three collections that I have visited—have already accepted the challenge; but there is plenty of room left for the rest of us.

LITERATURE CITED

1. Jack Williamson, "Science Fiction Comes to College," *Extrapolation* 12: 67–78 (May 1971).
2. Myres S. McDougal, Harold D. Lasswell, and Ivan A. Vlasic, *Law and Public Order in Space* (New Haven, Yale University Press, 1963).
3. Sam Moskowitz, "How Science Fiction Got Its Name." In his *Explorers of the Infinite* (Cleveland, World, 1963), pp. 313–333.
4. Anthony Boucher, "The Publishing of Science Fiction." In Reginald Bretnor (ed.), *Modern Science Fiction* (New York, Coward-McCann, 1953), p. 37.
5. Alastair Cameron, *Fantasy Classification System.* Privately printed, 1952.
6. Fred Lerner, "Cataloging and Classification of Science Fiction Collections," to be published in *Proceedings* of Secondary Universe IV. [Note: The Secondary Universe IV *Proceedings* was never published; instead, this essay was published in the journal *Special Collections,* and is reprinted in this book.]
7. Sidney Ives, personal communication, 1968.

Presented June 7, 1972, as a contributed paper, during SLA's 63rd Annual Conference in Boston.

The Cataloging and Classification
of Science Fiction Collections

Despite the increase in the number of science fiction collections in research libraries since the Clarkson Collection was donated to Harvard in 1955, very little attention has been paid to their cataloging and classification. Those which are primarily manuscript collections, such as those at Boston University and Syracuse University, are arranged according to the principles of archival management. The papers of a particular individual or organization are listed in card-files and descriptive brochures; and calendars are prepared for those whose extent warrants it. Books and periodicals are either regarded as adjuncts to the manuscript material, or are integrated into the rare book collection. In the latter case, descriptive cataloging is generally limited to the basic information required by the Anglo-American Cataloging Rules, and subject cataloging, if provided at all, is limited to the application of subject headings from the Library of Congress list.

Even in those collections consisting primarily or entirely of printed materials, cataloging receives minimal attention. Relationships between works, problems of anonymous or pseudonymous authorship, and peculiarities of publishing history are left to the bibliographical literature, which fortunately is voluminous in this field. Thematic bibliography of science fiction is much less advanced than enumerative bibliography: despite Sackett's call for a "Motif Index of Science Fiction" in 1960[1], neither amateur nor professional scholars have done much toward facilitating a subject approach to science fiction stories. Until recently, neither the bibliographical literature nor the subject headings applied in library catalogs have offered much help to the reader seeking stories using a particular setting, theme, or device.

The rules laid down for descriptive cataloging in the second edition of the Anglo-American Cataloging Rules are in most regards suitable for science fiction collections. Of the three levels of description outlined in AACR2, the third level, which is the most detailed, would be preferable for research collections. More detailed description might be warranted for unique items or for those substantially altered from their original condition (as by annotation, insertion of illustrations, or the like); but the need for title-page transcription or other painstaking distinctions of state and issue might be obviated by the publication of detailed descriptive bibliographies, to which reference might be made in notes to the catalog entries.[2]

Certain aspects of the publishing of science fiction deserve the cataloger's attention. The description of a science fiction book should indicate whether it is a deluxe hardcover, trade hardcover, book club, trade paperback, or mass-market paperback edition. The printing should also be identified, as there are often slight changes in text or artwork between printings. Cover, jacket, and interior artists should always be identified; and publishers' stock numbers and cover prices should be recorded. The role of editors and publishers in determining or influencing the content of many works should be borne in mind when establishing entries. Story series and other relationships between stories, including relationships between stories by different writers, should be indicated.

The literature of cataloging is full of complaints about the inability of subject catalogers to devise and maintain up-to-date lists of subject headings. Technological and social change, and the literature which they occasion, are inadequately represented by the terms in general library use. Indeed, there exists a prize-winning journal (the *Hennepin County Library Cataloging Bulletin*) whose primary purpose is the provision of appropriate subject headings and Dewey Decimal classification numbers for subjects of current interest.

Against this background there is little reason to suppose that a list of subject headings could be devised which would serve adequately to reflect the content of science fiction stories. Science fiction is, after all, an innovative literature whose entire reason for being is to anticipate developments which have not yet occurred.[3] The subject headings assigned to science fiction books by the Library of Congress are often incorrect, and in any event contribute very little to the library user's ability to find what he might be seeking.

The Library of Congress assigns subject headings to collections and anthologies, but not to novels.[4] The headings "Science Fiction, American," "Science Fiction, English," etc., are usually used. Occasionally an additional heading, such as "Immortality—Fiction" or "Wyoming—Fiction," is assigned to an anthology of stories on a particular theme.

Such headings as "Science Fiction, American" or "Science Fiction, English" do not consistently reflect with accuracy the nationality of the authors of the stories so described. Headings such as "Science Fiction, English—Translations from Russian" offer an access point which only a cataloger might think of employing, and throw doubt on just what the Library of Congress might mean by "English." Another unfortunate confusion arises from the Library of Congress's use of "Collections" to mean a group of stories written by different hands (the term is used in the same way in the Dewey Decimal Classification). Science fiction bibliographers usually call such works "anthologies," as distinguished from "collections" of stories by a singular writer or a team of writers in collaboration.

Headings such as "Science Fiction—Bibliography" or "Science Fiction—History" would be much more useful to readers were it not for the Library of Congress's practice of arbitrarily assigning to some of the secondary works headings such as "Science Fiction, American—Bibliography" or "Science Fiction, English—History and Criticism." In some cases "Fantastic Fiction" is used as a heading or part of one, offering a distinction which few bibliographers familiar with the literature of fantasy and science fiction would care to make.

In a specialized collection devoted to this literature, there seems little reason to attempt in a catalog any subject approach to the fiction. As scholarly interest arises in some particular area, bibliographies will be compiled and published; these will be more complete in their coverage than any guide to a single collection could be. Already the literature affords lists of stories about future wars[5], robots[6], and novels with female protagonists[7]; and such reference works as the *Science Fiction Encyclopedia*[8] and *Science Fiction: Contemporary Mythology*[9] offer subject approaches to novels and anthologies. Some such anthologies themselves contain listings of other stories on their central theme.

Since only a fraction of the bibliographical, critical, and historical writing about science fiction appears in book or pamphlet form, the effort made to provide subject cataloging for this material would reveal to the reader only a portion of the collection's resources, and would mislead him as to the amount and nature of the material available. While the extensive use of analytic entries for periodicals and composite works would alleviate this problem, it would duplicate the extensive indexing of this material provided by existing and projected bibliographies.

In short, while existing systems of subject cataloging are almost useless for science fiction collections, the extensive bibliographical literature of science fiction makes the effort and expense of subject cataloging unnecessary.

In addition to describing the physical form and intellectual content of the items in the collection, a library catalog must specify the location of each item. A library collection which is housed in closed stacks, with books being delivered to readers who have requested specific titles, does not require an elaborate classification scheme. Any system of identification which provides a unique address for each item in the collection will suffice. Books may be assigned serial numbers in order of accession; or, in a collection cramped for space, the physical size of each volume can determine its place on the shelves. So long as a good catalog is available, a reader seeking a specific book will be able to obtain what he wants.

In an open-stack library, where readers are permitted direct access to the collection as a whole, a more systematic arrangement of its contents is needed. Some scheme for bringing together similar materials would be helpful for the purposeful searcher and the casual browser alike. A carefully designed classification scheme can offer a valuable systematic approach to the collection (it can also be used to organize a classified catalog for a closed-shelf collection, or for any extensive science fiction bibliography).

Librarians have devised many classification schemes for both general and specialized collections. In the United States, the most widely used systems for general collections are the Dewey Decimal System (DDC) and the Library of Congress Classification (LC). Neither of these general classifications, nor such other schemes as the Universal Decimal Classification, the Bliss Bibliographic Classification, or the Colon Classification, meets the needs of a library specializing in science fiction. They are designed to cover the entire range of human knowledge and achievement; and of that immense range, science fiction forms a minute part.

Until very recently, neither the Dewey Decimal Classification nor the Library of Congress Classification provided any distinction between science fiction books and other works of fiction. Nationality, rather than literary genre or subject-matter, was the principle governing the subdivision of the fiction classes. In the Dewey system, American science fiction novels, collections, and anthologies were classified in 813 (American fiction), French ones in 843 (French fiction), Russian titles in 891.73, and so on. The Library of Congress would place an American title in PS (American literature), a French one in PQ, and a Russian one in PG—unless it chose to assign it to the PZ classification ("Fiction in English" and "Juvenile Literature").

With the 19th edition of the Dewey Decimal Classification (1979), specific classification numbers were provided for science fiction. The instructions given in Table 3 ("Subdivisions of Individual Literatures") call for the addition of "0876" (signifying, hierarchically, "Fiction of specific scopes and topics. Specific types of fiction. Adventure. Science") to the general number for fiction. Thus an American science fiction novel or story collection would be assigned 813.0876, and an English one 823.0876. The notation grows lengthier in the minor literatures: Canadian science fiction is 819.130876, and Russian—still a minor literature in the Procrustean framework of

Dewey—science fiction is 891.730876. These unwieldy numbers can grow to ludicrous lengths: an anthology of science fiction stories by Afro-American writers would be assigned a call number beginning with 813.0876080896073—to which would have to be added the Cutter number distinguishing the particular publication!

These impossibly long numbers might be advantageous in a classified catalog, or in a computerized bibliography (they would lend themselves to truncation, which would facilitate mechanized searching), but they would be difficult to use as guides to shelf location. Not only would they be almost impossible to remember during the walk from catalog to shelf, but they would be awkward to inscribe on the spine of a mass-market paperback.

Somewhat better provision is made in Dewey for books *about* science fiction. The technique of SF writing is assigned the number 808.3876, while general history and criticism falls under 809.3876. The history and criticism of the science fiction generated by specific literatures is classified under a number constructed by adding "09" to the number for that literature's science fiction novels. Unfortunately, this leads to such numbers as 891.793087609 (history of Ukrainian science fiction).

The Library of Congress classification provides specific class numbers only for science fiction "collections" (i.e., anthologies), historical and critical works, bibliographies, and books on the technique of science fiction writing. No numbers are provided for SF novels or story collections, except those for general fiction of the appropriate nationality and period.

Anthologies are classified within each major literature, and in the General Literature class, under "Collections...Prose (General). Special forms and topics, A–Z" or some similar wording. Historical and critical works fall under "History of...Literature. Prose...Prose fiction...Special topics, A–Z." The call numbers for anthologies and historical/critical studies are formed by adding a Cutter number (typically .S3 or .S35) to the catch-all "special topics" number; a second Cutter number indicates the author or editor of the books. Thus anthologies of science fiction from various literatures fall under PN6071.S33; American SF anthologies, PS648.S3; and anthologies of English science fiction, PR1309.S3. Science fiction history and criticism are classified under PN3448.S45 (general, except for recent works), PS374.S35 (American), and PR830.S35 (English). A similar classification is applied to anthologies and history/criticism of Australian, French, German, Russian, Spanish, and other science fiction.

Books on the technique of science fiction writing are classified in PN3377.5.S3, another "special topics" number. Bibliographies of science fiction are assigned similar numbers within LC's Z schedule. The Z schedule was the first part of the LC classification to be devised; it is almost purely arbitrary in its arrangement, and is scarcely suited to a general collection, much less a specialized one.

Very recently (since the publication of the 1978 edition of the PN, PR, PS, PZ schedule), the Library of Congress has made a more generous provision for books about science fiction. The PN3448.S35 number has been replaced by PN3443 and its subdivislons:

Prose.
Prose fiction.
Special kinds of fiction.
Science fiction.

PN3443   Periodicals, societies, etc.

     .2 Congresses

     .3 Exhibitions, museums, etc.

     .4 Encyclopedias, dictionaries

     .5 General works

     .6 Special topics (not A–Z)

     .7 Study and teaching Authorship. Technique, see PN3377.5.S3

     .8 History

This is certainly better than what preceded it. However, it is still insufficient for the classification of an extensive collection; libraries cannot realistically be expected to reclassify earlier titles into PN3443; and it does not appear that this new number is meant to replace the numbers provided for literary history and criticism of science fiction in the individual national literature schedules. So books about science fiction will continue to be scattered among the shelves of research libraries using the LC classification.

Moreover, the Library of Congress classification makes a mischievous provision for the application of alternative class numbers to many science fiction anthologies and historical/critical works. In addition to the Cutter number for "science fiction," Cutter numbers for such classes as the following may be found in the same "special topics" listings: Fantastic fiction, Interplanetary voyages, Mars (planet), Space flight to the moon, Utopias, and Venus (planet). It is entirely possible for an anthology of SF stories set on Mars to be separated by hundreds of mystery anthologies from the majority of the science fiction titles, or for a study of fantasy which includes science fiction to be shelved apart from a history of science fiction which does not so apparently mention fantasy.

The classification numbers provided in the Dewey and LC schedules can of course be combined with Cutter numbers for specific authors and titles to produce call numbers for a specialized collection of science fiction. But the necessity for distinguishing among multiple titles and editions within the output of each writer would produce inconveniently long call numbers. And the distinctive sub-topics allowed within a general classification scheme are inadequate to the needs of a large science fiction collection.

This problem is not unique to science fiction. Almost every large specialized library has found it necessary either to expand and adapt an existing general classification[10] or to invent a new one.[11] Many of these specialized classification systems are the result of several years' trial and error, and grew one step ahead of—or behind—the collections for which they were invented.

I know of no published classification scheme designed for science fiction collections. Alastair Cameron's fascinating *Fantasy Classification System*[12] is a scheme for classifying stories, rather than books. It is very valuable in its own right—among other things, it is the most elaborate ostensive approach to a definition of fantasy fiction that we have—but it cannot serve as a library classification.

Over the past ten years I have been developing what I call the Fantasy Collection Classification Scheme (FCCS). This is a system for the classification of a hypothetical library which is assembling a complete collection of the fantasy and science fiction literature. FCCS is designed to be compatible with the Library of Congress classification. It takes the form of a PX subclass of LC's class P ("Language and Literature").

The LC classification has no PX subclass; there is a void between PT and PZ. The PX ("Fantastic Literature") subclass falls logically between the "Literature" subclass PN through PT and the "Fiction and Juvenile Literature" subclass PZ.[13]

This compatibility would facilitate the rational arrangement of peripheral materials in a specialized science fiction collection. The users of such a collection would surely find it convenient to have ready access to a small reference library of general bibliographies, studies in literary history and criticism, basic texts on science and technology, and the like. It might also be desirable to collect the non-SF publications of science fiction writers, thus allowing the convenient study of the literary career of a Wells or an Asimov. All non-SF materials could be classified according to the published LC system, avoiding the confusion that often results when two dissimilar classifications are used in the same library.

Like the LC classification, the Fantasy Collection Classification Scheme is founded upon literary warrant: upon the nature and extent of the literature rather than a theoretical division of knowledge. But I have attempted to anticipate future developments in the literature, and to allow ample room to accommodate unanticipated trends.

As with descriptive cataloging, a classification scheme should take into account the peculiar patterns of writing, publishing, and collecting which have evolved in the case of science fiction. FCCS is based on three premises:

(1) Most students and collectors of science fiction recognize a close relationship between SF and other types of fantastic literature. Many science fiction writers have published heroic, weird, or whimsical fantasies, as well as tales based on scientific premises; and the "cognitive estrangement"[14] common to fantasy and science fiction leads both casual readers and serious scholars to think of them as aspects of the same literary genre. The commercial fiction marketplace, at least in the United States, has tended to view "fantasy" as a subclass of "science fiction," while SF historians have often described "science fiction" as a subclass of "fantasy".[15] No single definition of "science fiction" has ever gained universal acceptance; but there is a consensus that the term "science fiction" itself does not adequately describe the genre. FCCS treats science fiction as a subclass of fantastic literature.

(2) The organization of a fantasy collection should take into account patterns of writing and publishing peculiar to the genre. The close-knit and highly interactive nature of the fantasy field in most cases precludes the study of a single writer's work in isolation; accordingly, bibliographical and critical studies focusing on a single writer are classed with general bibliographical and critical works, rather than with the subject's own writings (as they would be in the LC classification). Similarly, the influence of editors and anthologists in shaping the field is reflected in the detailed provision made for the arrangement of the several types of anthologies.

(3) In a classification designed for the physical arrangement of literary artifacts (as opposed to one designed for the organization of bibliographic records) it is appropriate to take into account the physical properties of the materials being classified. Therefore, in several cases mass-market paperback publications are placed in a separate classification from hardcover books and trade paperbacks; and non-print materials are also separately classified. The justification for this lies in the physical awkwardness that would result from uncompromisingly ignoring the format of publication; it is based on the experience and practice of several collectors. (Libraries which find this separation by format repugnant can of course abridge this scheme to suit their preferences.)

A complete FCCS call number occupies three to five lines. The first two lines are occupied by "PX" and the specific classification number. Where books within a specific classification are arranged alphabetically by author (which should be assumed unless otherwise specified), the third line of the call number is the author's Cutter number, the fourth line is the Cutter number for the title, and the fifth line is the date (where necessary to identify edition). When a classification is subarranged alphabetically by title or theme, the third line of the call number is the Cutter number for that characteristic, the fourth line (if needed) identifies the author, and the fifth line the title or date, as necessary.

The classification schedule and tables for the Fantasy Collection Classification Scheme appear below as an appendix to this essay.[16]

APPENDIX—FANTASY COLLECTION CLASSIFICATION SCHEME

PX FANTASTIC LITERATURE

General works

1	Encyclopedias and handbooks
10	Dictionaries and glossaries
	Periodicals:
20	devoted entirely or primarily to fantasy (nonfiction)
25	issues of general periodicals containing fantasy (fiction and/or nonfiction)
30	Yearbooks
40	Societies
50	Congresses
60	Series. Monographs by different writers.
70	Principles of bibliography and librarianship as applied to fantasy collections
73	Acquisition of materials
75	Cataloging and classification
76	Indexing
77	Conservation of materials
81	Use of materials
90	Study and teaching (For technique of writing fantasy, see PX315–316)
91	Techniques of teaching fantasy courses
92	Lists of courses
	Course outlines and syllabi:
93	Collections
94	Colleges, A–Z
95	Schools, A–Z
96	Review books
97	Textbooks

100 *Bibliography of fantasy and secondary materials*

101	Bibliography of secondary materials
103	Bibliographies
105	Historical and critical works
106	Dissertations and theses
107	Book reviews
109	Translations

260	Advertising periodicals, by title, A–Z
(300)	*History and Criticism of Fantasy*
311	Definition of fantasy
315	Theory and technique of writing fantasy
316	Writers' organizations and workshops, A–Z (e.g., .C5 Clarion, .M4 Milford)
317	Literary awards and prizes
320	General history and criticism of fantasy
322	Epics and sagas
324	Heroic fantasy
326	Weird fantasy
332	Science fantasy. Science fiction
334	Utopian/dystopian fantasy
336	Satirical fantasy
338	Whimsical fantasy
342	Themes within fantasy stories
344	Specific themes, A–Z
346	Stories for special audiences
347	Juvenile readers
348	Other classes, A–Z
349	Literary circles, A–Z (e.g., .I6 Inklings, .L7 Lovecraft Circle)
(350)	History and criticism of fantasy, by medium
(356)	Printed books (Prefer PX320)
357	Individual publishers, A–Z
358	Periodicals
359	Individual periodicals, A–Z
360	Nonprint media
362	Motion pictures
363	Individual filmmakers, A–Z
364	Pictorial or plastic art
365	Individual artists, A–Z
366	Maps
367	Individual mapmakers, A–Z
368	Music
369	Individual composers, A–Z
370	Sound recordings
371	Individual performers, A–Z
372	Kits, realia, etc.
373	Individual producers, A–Z
374	Formats for touch-reading
375	Recordings for the blind or handicapped
376	Computer software
377	Individual producers, A–Z
378	Broadcasts
379	Individual producers, A–Z
380	Games, puzzles, etc.
381	Individual producers, A–Z
396	Other formats
398	Ephemera

History and criticism of fantasy, by writer

399	Biographical directories
399.5	Pseudonyms and anonyms
400	Individual writers, A–Z (Use Table I)
500	History and criticism of fantasy, by culture, ideology, or country of origin (Use Table II)

Fantasy fiction in printed form

1000	Magazines (periodicals devoted entirely or primarily to fantasy fiction), by title, A–Z (For nonfiction periodicals see PX20)

Anthologies of fantasy stories

1200	Stories selected from individual magazines, by magazine title, A–Z
1300	(The same, in mass-market paperback format)
1400	Anthologies published serially, by title, A–Z (e.g., .O7 Orbit)
1500	(The same, in mass-market paperback format)
1600	Award-winning stories, by award, A–Z (e.g., .N3 Nebula Award Stories)
1700	(The same, in mass-market paperback format)
1800	Stories selected by culture, ideology, or country of origin (Use Table II)
1900	(The same, in mass-market paperback format)
2000	Miscellaneous anthologies, by editor, A–Z
2100	(The same, in mass-market paperback format)
2200	Publishers' composite series, by publisher, A–Z (Within each publisher, by publisher's serial number, e.g., .A2 Ace Double Novels, .T8 Twayne Triplets)
2500	Novels and story collections (the work of a single writer or collaborative team), by author, A–Z
2700	(The same, in mass-market paperback format)

Fantasy fiction in nonprint form

3200	Motion Pictures (Use Table III)
3400	Pictorial or plastic art (Use Table III)
3600	Maps (Use Table III)
3800	Music (Use Table III)
4000	Sound recordings (Use Table III)
4200	Kits, realia, etc. (Use Table III)
4400	Formats for touch-reading (Use Table IV)
	Recordings for the blind or handicapped (See PX4000)
4600	Computer software (Use Table III)
	Broadcasts (See PX3200 or PX4000)
5000	Games, puzzles, etc., by producer, A–Z
5200	Microforms, videodiscs, etc. (Use Table III)
5600	Other formats (Use Table III)
5800	Ephemera, by producer, A–Z

(8000) *Fandom*

	General works
8001	Encyclopedias and handbooks
8010	Dictionaries and glossaries
8020	Periodicals and newsletters (For bibliographical, historical and critical periodicals, see PX20. For personal fanzines, see PX9000. For amateur press associations, see PX9200)

8030	Yearbooks
8100	Directories
8110-99	By country (Use Table II)
8200	Bibliography
8210-99	By country (Use Table II)
8300	History
8310-99	By country (Use Table II)
8400	Clubs and organizations
8401	World Science Fiction Society
8410-99	Other clubs and organizations, by country (Use Table II)
8500	Conferences and conventions
8501-99	World Science Fiction Convention (Use Table V)
8700	Other conferences and conventions
8710-99	By country (Use Table II)
9000	Fanzines (For bibliography of fanzines, use PX8200)
9100	By title, A–Z
9200	Amateur press associations, by name, A–Z (Use Table VI)

Table I

Cuttering for History and criticism of fantasy, by writer. Individual writers, A–Z. Add to PX400:

.A1A–Z	Bibliography, by compiler, A–Z
	Biography (Use .A4-.Z3) .
.A2A–Z	Autobiography, by title, A–Z
.A3A–Z	Letters, by editor, A–Z
.A4-.Z3	Criticism (including biography), by author, A–Z
.Z4-.Z8	Works, characters, etc.
.Z9A–Z	Relationship to other writers, by writer, A–Z (Prefer PX349 where appli-cable)

Table II

Cultural, ideological, and national treatment of fantasy. Add numbers below to base number as indicated in Classification Schedule (e.g., History and criticism of fantasy in Sweden, PX535).

1	Gender, sexual orientation, etc.
2	By gender, orientation, etc., A–Z (e.g., .L3 Lesbian)
3	Religion
4	By religion, A–Z (e.g., .C4 Christian, .M7 Moslem)
5	Political or social orientation
6	By orientation, A–Z (e.g., .L4 Libertarian, .S7 Socialist)
7	Racial or ethnic group
8	By group, A–Z (e.g., .B5 Black)
9	Other characteristics, A–Z (e.g., .B4 Blind)
	Nationality
10	North American
11	United States of America
12	Amerind, Inuit, etc.
13	Afro-American
14	Other ethnic, A–Z
15	Foreign-langua ge

16	Canada	
17		Anglophone
18		Francophone
19		Other
20	European	
21		British Isles
22		England
23		Scotland, Isle of Man
24		Wales, Cornwall
25		Ireland
26		German-speaking countries
27		Germany
28		Austria
29		Switzerland
30		Netherlands (including Frisian and Flemish)
31		Scandinavia
32		Denmark, Faeroe Islands
33		Iceland
34		Norway
35		Sweden
36		Finland
37		French-speaking countries
38		France
39		Belgium (for Flemish, see 30)
40		Italy
41		Spain
42		Portugal
43		Greece
44		Eastern Europe
45		Union of Soviet Socialist Republics
46		Russian
47		Ukrainian
48		Other Soviet nationalities, A–Z
49		Poland
50		Czechoslovakia
51		Hungary
52		Yugoslavia
53		Rumania
54		Bulgaria
55		Albania
56		Other European
57	Middle Eastern	
58		Arab countries (for Arabs, ethnic group, see 8.A7, for Arab countries of Africa, see 69–71)
59		Syria
60		Iraq
61		Lebanon
62		Jordan
63		West Bank and Gaza
64		Arabian Peninsula

65	Turkey	
66	Israel	
67	Iran	
68	African	
69		Arab countries of Africa
70		Egypt
71		Other countries, A–Z
72		Black Africa
73		By country, A–Z
74		Republic of South Africa
75	Asian	
76		India
77		By language, A–Z
78		Pakistan
79		Vietnam
80		Indonesia
81		China
82		Japan
83		Korea
84		Other countries, A–Z
85	Pacific	
86		Australia
87		New Zealand
88		Other countries, A–Z
89	Latin America	
90		Mexico
91		Central American and Caribbean countries
92		By country, A–Z
93		South American
94		Venezuela
95		Brazil
96		Argentina
97		Other countries, A–Z
98	Other countries, A–Z	
99	Extraterrestrial	

Table III

Fantasy fiction in nonprint form. Add numbers below to base number as indicated in Classification Schedule, as applicable (for example., PX4001, Bibliography of fantasy, issued as a sound recording).

1 Bibliography
3 History and criticism
10 Periodicals
12 Anthologies
25 Works by a single writer, producer, or collaborative team

Table IV

Formats for touch-reading. Add numbers below to base number as indicated in Classification Schedule.

	Braille
1	Bibliography
3	History and criticism
10	Periodicals
	Anthologies of fantasy stories
12	Stories selected from individual magazines, by magazine title, A–Z
14	Anthologies published serially, by title, A–Z
16	Award-winning stories, by award, A–Z
20	Other anthologies, by editor, A–Z
25	Novels and story collections, by author, A–Z
80	Fandom
90	Fanzines
91	By title, A–Z
92	Amateur press associations, by name, A–Z
	Moon type
93	Nonfictional materials
94	Periodicals
95	Anthologies
96	Novels and story collections
97	Other formats, by format, A–Z

Table V

World Science Fiction Convention. Add to base number PX8500 the number of the convention (e.g., PX8507, 7th World Science Fiction Convention) and the following:

0	History
.1	Official publications (i.e., those distributed to all Convention members)
.2	Semi-official publications (i.e., those produced by or under the authority of the Convention but not necessarily distributed to all members)
.3	Unofficial publications
.4	Special activities, A–Z (e.g., .A7 Art Show, .B2 Business meeting, .M2 Masquerade)
.8	Ephemera
.9	Rival or breakaway conventions

Table VI

Cuttering for Amateur Press Associations, by name, A–Z. Add to PX9200 (where .x is the Cutter number for the Association):

.x1	History
.x2	Membership lists
.x3	Bibliographies and indexes
.x5	Anthologies
.x6	Mailing bundles and postmailings
.x7	Unofficial mailings
.x8	Official organs
.x9	Miscellaneous publications

NOTES

1. S. J. Sackett, "A Motif Index for Science Fiction?" *Extrapolation 1* (May 1960): 38.

2. See AACR2, rule 1.7B15.

3. Alastair Cameron's *Fantasy Classification System* (St. Vital, Manitoba: Canadian Science Fiction Association, 1951) provides over 500 categories into which fantasy and science fiction stories might be classified by subject; yet not one of these categories is appropriate to a novel widely considered to be the most important science fiction novel of the last twenty years—Ursula Le Guin's *The Left Hand of Darkness*.

4. In recent years, headings have been suggested for some juvenile novels.

5. I. F. Clarke, *Voices Prophesying War 1763–1984* (London: Oxford University Press, 1966), pp. 227–249.

6. Patricia S. Warrick, *The Cybernetic Imagination in Science Fiction* (Cambridge: MIT Press, 1980), pp. 259–269.

7. George Fergus, "A Checklist of SF Novels with Female Protagonists," *Extrapolation* 18 (December 1976): 20–27.

8. Peter Nicholls, ed., *The Science Fiction Encyclopedia* (Garden City: Dolphin Books, 1979).

9. Patricia Warrick, Martin Harry Greenberg, and Joseph Olander, eds., *Science Fiction: Contemporary Mythology; The SFWA-SFRA Anthology* (New York: Harper & Row, 1978).

10. One of the most recent examples is Darlene Myers, "Proposed Expansion of the Library of Congress Classification Sections QA75 and QA76: A Draft," in *Computer Science Resources: A Guide to the Professional Literature,* compiled by Darlene Myers (White Plains, New York: Knowledge Industry Publications for the American Society for Information Science, 1981), pp. 335–344.

11. The Harvard Business School's Baker Library and Columbia University's Avery Architectural Library are examples.

12. See note 3, above.

13. This gap would also provide room for the construction of additional subclasses for other special literary genres, such as detective fiction, pornography, or westerns.

14. Darko Suvin describes science fiction as the "literature of cognitive estrangement" in his *Metamorphoses of Science Fiction: On the Poetics and History of a Literary Genre* (New Haven: Yale University Press, 1979), p. 4.

15. For example, Brian Aldiss, *Billion Year Spree: The True History of Science Fiction* (Garden City: Doubleday, 1973), p. 8.

16. I would like to acknowledge the helpful criticism and comments on FCCS supplied over the past decade by Hal W. Hall and Leslie Kay Swigart.

The Popularity of Science Fiction

Twenty years ago, a young Chicagoan named Earl Kemp conducted an informal survey asking a few dozen people, "Who Killed Science Fiction?" Three hundred fans at the 19th World Science Fiction Convention in Seattle applauded as he received a Hugo Award for his work.

Almost four thousand people gathered in Denver for the 39th World Science Fiction Convention, at which Hugos were awarded to a handful of the hundreds of SF books published during 1980. If science fiction is dying today, it is not of starvation.

In recent years, as many as one-sixth of all American fiction books published have been science fiction titles. Bookstores specializing in science fiction and fantasy exist in most major American cities. *Omni*, a glossy monthly mingling science fact and science fiction, has been one of the great success stories of twentieth-century magazine publishing. The creative and financial impact of *Star Wars* has reverberated throughout the entertainment industry, and even threatens to bring radio drama back into existence. The question to be asked these days is, "Who Revived Science Fiction—and Why?"

To a great extent the answer to that question is that American young people— teenagers and those in their twenties, male and female, white, brown, and black— have made science fiction one of the liveliest and most prosperous sectors of the contemporary publishing scene.

What has science fiction got to offer today's young reader? Several things:

Perspectives on change: Today's adolescent knows that the world into which he was born is not the same world in which he will live out his adult years. The one constant is change: rapid technological and social change. The psychological effects of this upon the unprepared adult can be devastating: the "future shock" of Alvin Toffler's phrase. Science fiction is based on the notion of change; and in SF stories we see men and women facing—and usually surviving—conditions radically different from our experience and often from theirs. Through reading science fiction stories teenagers can become accustomed to the idea of change and can become more confident about humanity's ability to meet the challenge it poses.

Alternative experiences: Many young people live in homogeneous communities. Even in large, multi-ethnic cities, a teenager may be virtually isolated from members of other cultures. Reading of any kind helps to surmount this isolation; but science fiction offers greater range than earthbound literature and of course is not constrained by the known facts of human history. Stories may be set in environments which have never existed on Earth—in libertarian utopias, matriarchal commonwealths, interspecies symbioses. Political philosophies or personal whimsies may be fleshed out into worlds for the reader's instruction or amusement.

Stories that matter: Science fiction writers have always been more interested in men and women who change things than in people to whom things just happen. The individual is seldom seen as a hapless pawn of fate predestined by genes or karma. And a writer seldom calls a new world into being merely to put a few ineffectual nonentities through their paces. At an age when they are preparing their own lives' work adolescents find in science fiction portrayals of men and women—often of their own age or only slightly older—whose work is important to themselves and to their societies; and who take joy in doing it and doing it well.

Vivid writing and action: Today's science fiction is incomparably more literate than the stories in the first SF pulp magazines. But one aspect of the pulp heritage still looms large in contemporary science fiction: the attention paid to grabbing and holding the reader's attention. Seldom is storytelling subordinated to prose style; yet SF writers have distinctive, easily recognizable narrative voices and their vocabulary is copious. (So is the reader's: science fiction writers have mastered the technique of giving their readers, between the lines, the facts and concepts they need to follow the story. Science fiction reading is the most painless vocabulary builder I know.) The action in a science fiction story may be more cerebral than physical; but the reader is made to feel the excitement of solving the hero's problem—whether it be correcting a technical malfunction in a communications satellite or saving the population of an entire galaxy.

One of the reasons for science fiction's liveliness is that it has been essentially an amateur literature. Most of its writers wrote science fiction because of their love for the genre rather than as a livelihood. It didn't pay as well as other types of literature. Only in the last decade have more than a handful of writers been able to make a living from science fiction; and many of these derive much of their income from stories first published forty years ago. The majority of science fiction writers have always been part-timers; professional writers who make the bulk of their income from literary activities in other fields but like science fiction for its speculative opportunities and intellectual excitement, or working scientists, engineers, doctors, lawyers, teachers, librarians, who produce the occasional story or novel for fun, and a little pocket money.

The love of science fiction has brought many of its writers and readers together into a tightly knit community. Science fiction Fandom represents a relationship of writer to reader unprecedented and unmatched in popular literature. It has spawned a substantial number of leading writers, critics, and scholars; and it has taken on a life of its own as an independent subculture which would doubtless continue to exist even were the writing and publishing of science fiction to cease entirely. Those active in Fandom made up at any time only a small proportion of the science fiction readership; but Fandom provided the environment in which science fiction developed as a distinguishable literature.

Science fiction, of course, is not a phenomenon exclusive to the twentieth century. Some historians have tried to find its roots in the ancient literatures of India, Babylonia, and Greece, while even conservative students of the genre find unmistakable examples as early as the first part of the nineteenth century. The theme of science as an agent of change served many of that century's leading writers: Hawthorne, Poe, Melville, Kipling, Doyle, and Wells all wrote science fiction stories and published them in respectable periodicals. And in the despised subliterature of the dime novel, stories of fabulous inventions captivated a wide audience.

But it was not until the dime novels evolved into the pulp magazines that an identifiable literature of fictionalized scientific speculation emerged. The reader seeking this kind of story had to search through the general fiction magazines and the bookshops and libraries in the hope of finding it—until that day in April 1926 when a magazine called *Amazing Stories* first appeared.

Hugo Gernsback didn't consider his science-oriented publication to be a pulp magazine. He avoided the standard pulp format, and modeled *Amazing Stories* on the science-hobbyist magazines from which it evolved. But it found its place among the other all-fiction magazines on the nation's newsstands; and the pulp chains, always seeking new formats in which to reap the benefits of economies of scale, soon gave it imitators clothed in the garish covers and untrimmed pages that typified the pulp magazine.

So now stories about science and technology had a market and a name—and an identification, in critical and popular mind alike, with a commercially inspired literature with no pretensions to social importance or lasting artistic value.

But there was a significant difference between science fiction and other pulp literatures. To many of its readers, science fiction was more than merely light reading or escape literature: it was a vehicle for ideas—scientific ideas and, to some extent, social ideas. Many of these readers were young men whose family circumstances (many were the sons of immigrants) or economic conditions (the 1930s were the period of the Great Depression) had kept them out of college. So they sought their education at the public library or the corner newsstand. The letter columns of the science fiction magazines gave them a forum in which to criticize both the stories and the ideas on which they were based; editors encouraged this, for it gave them a way of filling pages at no cost to their skimpy budgets. Readers began to correspond among themselves and in larger cities to form science fiction cubs. Most of these early fans aspired to write science fiction, and a great many of today's leading science fiction writers were among the active fans of those early days.

In fanzines and at conventions, through correspondence and club meetings, science fiction readers, writers, and editors created a provincial atmosphere which nurtured the literature. New writers emerged who had read the stories of their predecessors and who were able to take their ideas a step further. Literary standards improved as well, with editors such as John Campbell demanding competence in storytelling and readers expecting a more journeymanlike level of English prose. While the outside world took little notice, a common pool of techniques and conventions was being created, and scores of newcomers were serving their apprenticeships.

When the atomic bomb shocked Americans into realizing the impact of scientific discovery and technological change, science fiction began to receive a much higher level of attention from the mainstream. New markets came into being: juvenile and adult books from trade publishers, mass magazines such as the *Saturday Evening Post*, and national radio and television. But whereas television and paperback books helped to kill off the pulp magazines, the science fiction audience sought more from its reading than these media were able to offer. Science fiction magazines continued—there are several still being published today—providing a paying market for apprentice writers, as well as the continuity offered by editorials, book reviews, and letter columns.

Today, many of those who are in a position to make judgments about literature are people who grew up reading science fiction. The boundaries between science fiction as a category of commercial fiction publishing and science/technology as a theme for mainstream fiction are eroding. But just as there is something uniquely Canadian about the stories of a Margaret Atwood or Alice Munro, so the science fiction of Asimov and Heinlein, of Delany and Le Guin, of Benford and Varley shows the marks of the shared experiences from which it grew.

In too many libraries, science fiction is regarded as too unimportant to warrant careful selection. Some simply subscribe to Doubleday's monthly offering or buy paperbacks at random from a local newsstand or bookstore. There are many libraries, of course, in which the task of selection is delegated to a staff member with an ardent interest in science fiction; and others rely upon the advice of specialist reviewers in *Booklist* and *Library Journal*. But none of these methods is likely to build a science fiction collection representative of either the best work in the field or the leading trends in contemporary science fiction.

A collection development strategy for a small science fiction collection should take into account two premises: that science fiction books are individual works of literature, rather than interchangeable chunks of popular culture; and that there is an incongruous timelessness about good science fiction stories. The shelf life of a science fiction novel or story collection is substantially greater than that of the typical mainstream volume; titles first published in the 1940s are constantly reprinted, and avidly read by readers whose parents weren't even born when they first appeared. It may be the occupational hazard of science fiction writers to have their stories overtaken by events; but that does not seem to have much of an impact upon their readability. And science fiction readers usually have distinct favorites among writers, and search diligently for their books.

Fortunately for librarians unfamiliar with science fiction, there exists a voluminous literature of history, bibliography, and criticism. From the hundreds of books *about* science fiction, I would nominate these five as being most useful for librarians:

Neil Barron's *Anatomy of Wonder* has just been published in a revised and expanded second edition. Its historical and descriptive accounts of American and foreign science fiction provide a wealth of reliable information in a small amount of space. Extensive annotated bibliographies identify the major works from the various countries and historical periods. In addition to novels, collections, and anthologies, there is coverage of research aids for teachers, librarians, and scholars. And a carefully assembled "Core Collection Checklist" provides an excellent tool for evaluating or planning a library's science fiction collection.

In *A Reader's Guide to Science Fiction*, Baird Searles and his colleagues from New York's Science Fiction Shop provide a convenient and inexpensive guide to the leading writers of modern science fiction and their works. Two features make this guide especially useful to the librarian new to science fiction: the article on each writer suggests others whose stories might appeal to the same readership; and "The 5 Parsec Shelf" lists fifty titles which form a basic collection of which any library might be proud.

The Science Fiction Encyclopedia, edited by Peter Nicholls, devotes almost seven hundred pages to SF writers, films, magazines, and institutions. Particularly valuable are the 175 thematic articles exploring science fiction's treatment of anti-intellectualism, dystopias, religion, sex, etc. Each of these identifies major stories using its theme, greatly facilitating the use of science fiction in classes or assignments in science or social studies.

In order to gain a modest historical perspective one might read *Billion Year Spree,* Brian Aldiss's "True History of Science Fiction"; and the critical essays collected in *SF: The Other Side of Realism,* edited by Thomas D. Clareson, give a good cross section of leading approaches to the evaluation and analysis of the genre.

Should these five books pique the librarian's interest, there are a great many more: the publishing of books *about* science fiction is a phenomenon even more impressive than the commercial success of SF itself. The section on "Research Aids" in *Anatomy of Wonder* will suggest further titles. But the best way to learn about modern science fiction is to get hold of half a dozen good SF books and dive into them. Don't be discouraged by one or two which seem unreadable or incomprehensible or just plain uninteresting. Science fiction is a house of many mansions, and even among its most avid readers there are few (if any) who like all of it.

Given a fair trial, the reasons for science fiction's popularity among young men and women should become evident. Even if he or she cannot find any personal interest in the genre, the librarian who understands today's young people should be able to see why they read science fiction.

BOOKS MENTIONED

Aldiss, Brian W. *Billion Year Spree: The True History of Science Fiction.* Doubleday, 1973.

Barron, Neil (ed.). *Anatomy of Wonder: A Critical Guide to Science Fiction,* 2nd ed. New York: Bowker, 1981.

Clareson, Thomas D. *SF: The Other Side of Realism: Critical Essays on Modern Fantasy and Science Fiction.* Bowling Green University Popular Press, 1971.

Nicholls, Peter (ed.). *The Science Fiction Encyclopedia.* Doubleday/Dolphin, 1979.

Searles, Baird (ed.). *A Reader's Guide to Science Fiction.* Avon, 1979.

Farewell to Alexandria

Farewell to Alexandria. In a book with that title, Daniel Gore once argued that the traditional goal of an academic library—to provide its users with all the literature that they would need for their scholarship and teaching—is no longer an attainable one. Continuing growth is impossible; instead the college or university library should strive for a steady-state collection. The quality of a library should be measured by its selectivity, not its completeness. Obsolete and esoteric materials should be obtained through interlibrary loan, presumably from specialized literary archives. The ancient library of Alexandria, which set out to collect all the literature of the world, can no longer be the model for even the most ambitious of librarians.

I'm beginning to wonder if I don't need to adopt a similar philosophy with regard to my own science fiction collection. Twenty years ago I harbored dreams of collecting every science fiction and fantasy book ever published. This was of course an impossible ambition; even disregarding all that had been published before I began collecting, there was no way that I could afford to buy every trade hardcover and small press book that came out. For a year or two I maintained a standing order with a mail-order dealer for every new SF and fantasy paperback, but this proved unsustainable: I had neither the room nor the interest to justify receiving much of what came each month in the mail. More recently I have found myself on several publishers' review lists, and so an ever-increasing stream of books—hardcover as well as paperback—finds its way to my doorstep.

Life is short, and shelving is finite. I realized that I would never assemble the definitive collection of science fiction, so I discarded variant printings of the same book. Then one day I decided that I didn't need horror fiction, nor did I want the incomplete copies of endlessly derivative fantasy trilogies that had found their way into my collection. For that matter, I had no use for complete ones; so I purged my shelves of every paperback whose title or cover showed any sign of elf or dwarf, wizard or swordsman, dragon or unicorn. I found it a tremendously liberating experience. Once having thrown off the shackles of completism, I found myself wondering how much further I could go.

Straight science fiction was next. There were a lot of books that I had never read and never would read. Some were movie or television novelizations, others more original hackwork. I was careful here: no true connoisseur of science fiction should be without at least one example of Pel Torro's handiwork; and for that matter, no one who writes for young adult librarians should be too fastidious about Xanth novels. As a sometime historian I needed to be sure of having to hand some materials whose value is more documentary than aesthetic. So I kept a token Perry Rhodan novel, and I didn't entirely strip my shelves of horror.

And there were other considerations. I certainly wasn't going to throw out or give away books that were autographed or inscribed to me; or books by my friends; or sentimental favorites. Some books that I wouldn't ever have expected to read aroused

69

my interest because of recommendations from valued friends or trusted critics; others might find their way into a future *VOYA* column or historical essay. All that notwithstanding, a lot of paperbacks have been sent down from Worcester Avenue to the Gates Memorial Library.

Hardcover books are another matter. One wall of our living room is lined with bookshelves, and these are filled with science fiction, fantasy, and horror literature, in hardcover or trade paperback. There's no space for more books, save what I create by stashing less-favored ones behind those on display. Even that ruse won't buy me more than a few months.

Getting rid of hardcover books will be an especially wrenching experience. Paperbacks aren't *really* books, or so I can manage to convince myself; but covered boards and a dust wrapper portend *literature*. How should I choose the ones to sacrifice? Do I discard my old Science Fiction Book Club editions—and sweep *The Foundation Trilogy* and *Stranger in a Strange Land* from my shelves? Do I remove some of the less interesting titles from previous months' review packages—and risk losing the first edition of the next Heinlein's debut novel? Should I keep books I have read and enjoyed, for the pleasure of someday reading them again, or should they be sacrificed to make room for new books I might like to read someday? In short, to what purpose should that wall of bookshelves be consecrated?

I've played the old game of "let's define science fiction" in my time, and I challenge anyone reading this to top my definition. "Science fiction is the stuff on the bookshelves along my living room wall." Yes, it's a variant on Damon Knight's "It [science fiction] means what we point to when we say it," but I like a definition to be, well, more definite. And in that definition I see a possible answer to my quandary.

Perhaps my goal should be to use that finite space—it can hold perhaps five hundred books—to define science fiction in a sort of indefinite way. Or rather, a nondefinitive sort of way; that is, to create an ostensive definition that reflects all the facets of the science fiction field: its history, its ambiguities, its destiny. This needn't be an impersonal definition, by any means. One of the most important aspects of the science fiction field is the role played by idiosyncrasies of taste, and how better to illustrate that than with some of mine? So Keith Roberts is safe, and Ellen Kushner, and Avram Davidson, and R. A. Lafferty. Sentiment guarantees a few places: the Asimov books my parents brought me back from Israel, written in Hebrew but autographed in Yiddish; *The Man in the High Castle*, which won the Best Novel Hugo at my first Worldcon; Janet Kagan's *Mirabile*. And there's history (*The Dark Descent*, *The Astounding Science Fiction Anthology*) and plain merit (*The Book of Skulls*; *Little, Big*; *The Malacia Tapestry*).

If such a collection were a work of art, its title would be "What Science Fiction Means to Me." And why should a collection *not* be a work of art, and minimalist art at that? Consider the beauty of a Zen garden. Perhaps I shall join Daniel Gore in bidding farewell to Alexandria. It would not be an easy decision, but it might be a liberating one. Wish me luck.

An Imperfect Vermonter

Twenty-one years ago I moved to Vermont, more or less by accident. It didn't take me long to fall in love with the place, and my wife and daughter share that feeling. I hope that some of these pieces will explain why.

A long time ago I realized that I could never be a successful wine snob. Life is too short, and there are too many wines. Instead I resolved to learn the single-malt Scotches. They offer the complexity of flavor and the topographic idiosyncrasy of fine wine, but there are only one hundred and sixteen of them. A man might reasonably hope to learn them in a lifetime, and I've made a desultory start. The state of Vermont, a little over nine thousand square miles in area, offers a similar opportunity to appreciate the complexities and idiosyncrasies of a small but varied universe. I've made a desultory start there, too. "Vermonting" gives some idea of what might be found in a day's wandering.

The Vermont landscape arouses fierce protectionist sentiments in those who love it. We have strict laws regulating outdoor advertising, taxes that inhibit the speculative subdivision of open land, and governmental policies that discourage suburban sprawl. But these do not cover every threat to the Vermont environment, and there are times when an aroused citizenry must take matters into its own hands. "Proceedings and Transactions of the Vermont Commission on Tackiness" tells the story of one such citizens' crusade. It appeared (along with "Vermonting") in *Lofgeornost* #36 (August 1994).

It's not just her landscape that endears Vermont to so many of us. Her institutions and her people set the state apart. Some of that distinctiveness even spills over into the few corners of New Hampshire untainted by rampant development. On our wanderings through the North Country we have encountered several curious museums in unexpected settings. I describe two of them in "Uncle Bounce, I'll Miss You," which was written for *Lofgeornost* #32 (August 1993).

One encounters science fiction readers in the most unlikely places. I wasn't really surprised when a plumber who came to fix a leaky bathtub offered an astute evaluation of the Sprague de Camp novels I had on a nearby bookshelf. But I hadn't expected to spend an hour talking about science fiction with the governor of Vermont. "An Evening with Richard Snelling" appeared in *Lofgeornost* #4 (November 1982).

The late Governor Snelling wasn't the only Vermonter to see the relevance of science fiction to public affairs. As "The Vermont Bicentennial" suggests, SF has won a place in political discourse in Vermont. I wrote this piece in 1991, but it appears here for the first time.

71

Vermonting

It was a beautiful, clear, warm Saturday in early June, so naturally we went Vermonting. The word wasn't in my vocabulary before that morning, but there's no better to describe the activity: pick out some nominal destination, grab as recent a state highway map as you can find, hop in the car, and go. There are really only two rules to it. Keep off the interstate as much as possible, and stop anywhere you run across something interesting. Well, maybe there's a third: don't worry if you never actually get to the place you started out for.

Our nominal goal was the Old Stone House, a museum in the Northeast Kingdom town of Brownington, just a few miles south of the Quebec border. Ninety minutes on I-91 will take you there, but that's not playing the game. And think of what you'd miss.

For starters, there's the old bridge abutment that marks the long-abandoned right-of-way of the Montpelier & Wells River, a railway built by incorrigible optimists who reckoned that a profit could be made hauling milk and eggs from the hardscrabble farms of Orange County to the Boston & Maine railhead. This delusion became untenable fifty years ago, but if you know where to look enough remnants exist to conjure up a picture of life in a countryside so remote that the mixed train to Barre was the highway to civilization.

When I was a boy, weekend drives would sometimes include a visit to one of the model homes that dotted the evolving suburban landscape. Vermont's answer to the Levittown model is a large log structure beside Route 302 in Groton. I don't expect that we'll be leaving Worcester Avenue any time soon, but it's fun to imagine living in a log cabin just off a dirt road somewhere in the hills. Cathedral ceilings, a great stone fireplace, varnished smooth pine walls: there's something the antithesis of suburbia about it. But I'm not quite ready for the true country life of dry wells, backed-up septic systems, and four-wheel drive. I don't have to own a hillside to enjoy looking at one.

Driving through the woods, I often see lupins and day lilies, telltale reminders that one hundred fifty years ago Vermont was three-fourths farmland and one-fourth forest. Today it's the other way around, and many a stonewall through the woods testifies that some Vermont hill farmer found better land out west. We saw no day lilies this day, but another signal reminded us that the wild things reclaim their own. "Moose crossing next three miles" is not a sign you would have seen in Vermont ten years ago. But the moose have been working their way down country, following highway medians and railroad rights-of-way; and drivers watch carefully for their bulk, knowing the deadly danger of crashing into half a ton of moose at highway speeds. I've yet to spot one, but whenever I see a "Moose Crossing" sign I slow down and hope.

Whatever the day lacked in day lilies, it more than made up for in dandelions. By the dozen on your lawn the dandelion is an obnoxious weed; by the tens of thousands in a roadside meadow they are a flower of great beauty. Elizabeth was delighted by the sight of them, and demanded that we stop the car so that she might photograph them. From a hilltop in Cabot we could see carpets of dandelions leading the eye to the bulk of Camel's Hump and Mount Mansfield in the western distance. A few Holsteins, unconcerned with the grandeur of their backdrop, added just the homely touch the scene demanded. The Vermont landscape is an artifact of the dairy cow, and it's as well to have her in evidence when admiring it.

The Cabot Creamery is another artifact of the dairy cow, and we stopped in to see the transformation of fluid milk into butter and cheese. Like many another food processor in Vermont, Cabot has exploited its attraction to tourists. A gift shop is stocked with a bewildering variety of Vermont-made foodstuffs: not only the inevitable cheeses, pickles, preserves, and maple products, but also an improbable variety of salsas identified as "hecho en Vermont." I'm delighted to see all this. I can buy all this stuff more cheaply at the local co-op; but the fact that it's all there for me to buy means that the future of Vermont agriculture, and with it the future of the Vermont countryside, is less dependent on the dairy industry.

I was equally reassured to see that a favorite part of my past is still flourishing in downtown Marshfield. (It's admittedly a stretch to refer to the cluster of houses, official buildings, and general stores concentrated along a small strip of Route 2 as downtown anything, but then I often wonder at a Long Islander's reaction to the "thickly settled" signs that warn Vermont drivers that they are approaching an area where there are houses in sight of one another.) To my delight Rainbow Sweets was still in business as a combination bakery and cafe. One might not expect to encounter an Argentine empanada in rural Vermont, but theirs was excellent; and their pastries lived up to my fond memories of them. Rainbow Sweets was a two-minute detour off the forty-minute drive from Montpelier to the old granite quarry where I used to go skinny-dipping, and on many a hot summer afternoon I would recover from my aquatic exertions with a high-calorie restorative. The folks who run the place professed to remember the cake I once had them bake for one of my Queen's Birthday parties—a large yellow sheet cake whose border was frosted with equal numbers of white and red roses. (The Queen's Birthday is hardly a time to take sides!)

Working our way northward, I tried a shortcut to East Craftsbury. Like most of my dirt-road shortcuts, this led to our getting lost. The road we were traveling ended at a T-intersection, with nobody in sight except for a small herd of large animals. At first I thought they might be beefalo, a cross between bison and beef cattle that is gaining in popularity in Vermont. Its lean meat commanding a premium price, beefalo offers an alternative livelihood to dairy farming—and you don't have to get up at 4:30 to milk them. But this hypothesis proved untenable. Such a hybrid would no doubt be sterile, and the presence of two small calves that looked exactly like their mothers in miniature suggested that this was not the case. Elizabeth thought these creatures were cute, which is not the adjective I would have applied to such massive accumulations of hamburger on the hoof; she insisted on taking their pictures.

Still at a loss as to which direction to take, I headed right only to find that the road soon petered out. So I gingerly turned the car around, and a hundred yards after the shaggy herd we encountered a woodchuck in the field to our right. "Woodchuck" in Vermont sometimes refers to a large rodent, but just as often it means a native Vermonter, preferably of a crusty disposition. This woodchuck was of the latter kind, and I was careless with my phrasing when I addressed him.

"Can you tell me if this road goes to East Craftsbury?"

He looked at me, then glanced at our car and its green Vermont license plate. "You know the answer to that one."

"Let me rephrase that," I said. "Is this the road to East Craftsbury?"

He allowed that it was, and further enlightened us as to the beasts in the adjoining field. These were Highland cattle, a Scottish breed; and just that evening, watching a BBC serial called "Strathblair" set on a Perthshire hill farm, we saw them in their native habitat.

We did in fact find our way to East Craftsbury, where we paused briefly at the John Woodruff Simpson Memorial Library. One of two public libraries in the little town of Craftsbury, it boasts a collection that testifies to the erudition as well as the generosity of the family Simpson, and to the fondness for literature that's as old a Vermont tradition as the dairy cow. It's open at unusual times: Saturday afternoons, an hour just after noon on Sunday, and two hours each Wednesday evening. But this is not entirely idiosyncratic. Just after church lets out is a convenient time to exchange books; and no doubt Wednesday evenings were carefully chosen to accommodate the Craftsbury social calendar.

(The social life of Craftsbury runs to its own rhythm. About eighteen years ago I was showing a visitor around northern Vermont, and as we passed through East Craftsbury I noticed that the lights were on in the library. This was a curious thing to see on New Year's Day, so I stopped to see if in fact the building was open. It was; it had not occurred to anyone to suspend normal hours of operation for the holiday. When I explained that my companion and I were librarians, we were told to go next door, where Miss Jean, the elderly daughter of the library's namesake, was holding Open House. We were greeted warmly, although nobody present had ever heard of either of us.)

We finally found our way to Brownington, arriving there just in time to get a slightly abbreviated version of the museum tour. The Old Stone House was built by the Rev. Alexander Twilight to serve as a dormitory for the academy he ran; as it drew its students from all over Orleans County, some accommodation was needed for them. Twilight was a graduate of Middlebury College, and is believed to be the first American of African descent to receive a college degree, and the first to sit in a state legislature. His color did not seem to hamper his personal or professional life; his neighbors sent him to represent them in the General Assembly. (Though there have been occasional incidents, racism does not seem to be one of Vermont's major sins, and people of color have generally got along reasonably well here. So far as I know, Vermont is the only state with more African Americans in its legislature than in its prisons. The last time I checked, the ratio was three to two: three legislators, two prisoners.)

The building has been turned into the Orleans County historical museum. Each of its former sleeping rooms is dedicated to one of the county's towns and maintained by a local literary or historical society: my favorite is the Book and Thimble Club, which represents the Town of Orleans. The kitchen, dining area, and library represent the building's original function, as do such artifacts as a dugout bathtub and walls decorated with student graffiti. It's a modest collection, no competition for the Shelburne Museum; but it helps to keep alive the remembrance of days when Vermont could make its way with little recourse to the wider world.

And from there it was a straight shot down I-91, past Lyndonville, St. Johnsbury, and Bradford. Ninety minutes later we were sitting round our dinner table, back in our own little corner of Vermont.

Proceedings and Transactions of the Vermont Commission on Tackiness

Soon after I moved to Montpelier I got into the habit of driving around the Vermont countryside whenever the opportunity offered. One day a friend and I were exploring the Northeast Kingdom, a remote part of the state where white churches and red barns still dominated the built environment. But their domination was not complete. A few miles east of St. Johnsbury we were astonished to discover a ranch house painted lavender. It would have been appalling enough in a New Jersey suburb; it was entirely out of place in Caledonia County.

Naomi and I agreed that such tastelessness should not go unacknowledged. Just as passers-by might be warned of an unsafe building by a condemnation notice, the aesthetic safety of passing motorists should be protected. The situation demanded a sign proclaiming, "These premises have been declared tacky by the Vermont Commission on Tackiness."

Unfortunately, this particular commission had somehow been overlooked by the designers of Vermont's governmental structure. In the spirit of Ethan Allen, who once proclaimed that the newly established Republic of Vermont would be "governed by the laws of God and of Pennsylvania, until we shall have time to frame better ones," we decided to constitute the Vermont Commission on Tackiness without recourse to established authority. We spread the word among our circle in Montpelier that the Commission was about to begin its business.

As we were a most informal organization—we had not troubled to inform state government of our existence, and state government had not troubled to subsidize our activities, essential though these were to the common good—we had no official meeting place. This was no problem; we held our deliberations wherever two or more of us were assembled. We chose the Heritage office complex, a pair of cheaply built brick structures on River Street that housed some of the more peripheral state agencies, as our honorary headquarters—a designation that spared us any obligation to go near the place.

We might not have an office, but we did have an agenda. We would celebrate tackiness, whether embodied in architecture or manifested in word or deed, by releasing to an awaiting press our selections of those aspects of Vermont life most deserving of our recognition. In order that Commission members might have some badge of office, we resolved to wear thumbtacks in our lapels. (This improvement upon the yellow map pins affected by members of Mensa allowed us to bear witness to the inherent tackiness of *that* organization.) We were ready to go forth and discover tackiness wherever it disfigured Vermont.

And once we discovered it—what then? As we would need to assemble to report and evaluate our findings, we decided to hold a party to mark the occasion. Naturally it would be a tacky party. We would wear the tackiest clothes we could find, serve the tackiest refreshments we could imagine—artificial dairy toppings and pasteurized process cheese spreads were mentioned heavily in this discussion—and of course play tacky party games.

But it never happened. As we vied with one another to suggest the ultimate in tackiness, the party was evolving into one of those shared dreams whose realization could never possibly match our imagination of it. The fun of a tacky party—for that matter, the fun of the Vermont Commission on Tackiness—was all in the thinking and talking about it, not in the doing of it. We were wise enough to understand this, and by some unspoken consensus none of us ever tried to fix a specific time or place.

And soon summer was upon us, and we found other ways of celebrating our love for Vermont and our enjoyment of each other's company. Contra dances and picnics and country walks diverted us from all our tacky thoughts. If no lasting good came from our work, no harm came either. Vermont has managed to survive without a Commission on Tackiness—and the last time I drove eastward from St. Johnsbury on Route 2, that house was painted white.

Uncle Bounce, I'll Miss You

A few weeks ago Elizabeth asked if we might visit the Fairbanks Museum again. I was in the mood for a journey northwards, so we drove the seventy-two miles to St. Johnsbury. I have always enjoyed that museum, a barrel-vaulted throwback to the days when museums were attics first and classrooms second. And what a splendid attic it is!

The Fairbanks family made their money by manufacturing the world's best platform scales, and in proper New England fashion they spent a good deal of it embellishing their town. In addition to the natural history museum that bears their name, their imprint may be found in the elegant St. Johnsbury Athenaeum, housing one of Vermont's best public libraries as well as a fine collection of Hudson River School paintings, and in several of the handsome churches that line Main Street. But it is the Fairbanks Museum and Planetarium that draws outlanders into St. Johnsbury.

The main hall of the museum is filled with dead animals: some in lifelike dioramas; others, carefully labeled, in glass cases; and some hidden away in wooden drawers, immune from the scrutiny of all but the resolutely curious. The best-designed exhibits are of native Vermont creatures, but the ones that most fascinate me are the systematic arrangements of a region's fauna. I had always thought that a parrot was a parrot; the Creator's greater interest in the subject is evident from the multiplicity of species along the north wall. There are scores of hummingbird species in the New World, and the Fairbanks has them all. Even when the display is episodic rather than exhaustive, there is the thrill of seeing a creature that has featured prominently in a favorite story. And the animals in the Fairbanks Museum have one advantage over their colleagues in zoos: they are on full display, whenever the building is open; one need not attempt vainly to discern some evidence of life in a barely visible ball of brownish-gray fur tucked into a corner of a dimly lit cage.

The mezzanine that overlooks the main floor has its treats as well. There's a little bit of everything: a small cuneiform tablet, a Civil War soldier's sewing kit, a Malay kris, campaign buttons from forgotten elections. Some of these artifacts were brought home by globe-trotting Vermonters; others are cast-offs from larger collections. There's a certain satisfaction to knowing that one's curiosity about Babylonian writing or oriental weaponry can be at least partially assuaged locally: most people need to see only one clay tablet in a lifetime. To me, the real exhibit is the idea of the museum itself, what the miscellany of its collection tells about the good folk of St. Johnsbury, who manufactured platform scales, went to Africa as missionaries or to Japan as traders, and celebrated civic occasions with band concerts and public oratory. The Fairbanks Museum collects animals and objects from around the world, but it is really an expression of the purest sort of exuberant Americana.

Alas, another exuberant monument to New England's curiosity about the world is no more. The Morse Museum is closed forever, its contents dispersed at auction. Whether the Morse family no longer had the resources or the interest to maintain it, or whether they realized that Warren, New Hampshire, was a bit off the beaten track for such an eclectic collection, I do not know. I do know how disappointed I was to learn that Uncle Bounce's house had been pulled down.

Thirty-five years ago, one of my favorite books was a story called *The Dagger, the Fish, and Casey McGee.* Casey was a boy of ten or twelve, sent to spend the summer with his Uncle Bounce, a world traveler whose house was filled with strange and wondrous things acquired in the most improbable places. The plot had something to do with a band of foreign villains who coveted one of Uncle Bounce's treasures—no doubt it was either a dagger or a fish—but that wasn't what enthralled me. It was the house itself, and the jumble of exotica that made every journey from one room to another an adventure; and to this day I dream of living in a house like that.

The first time I stumbled across the Morse Museum, I realized that I had found the next best thing to Uncle Bounce's house. The Morse family had made their money in the mass production of shoes; had spent it traveling around the world, in the days when natives were natives and animals were there to shoot at; and had built a stone museum in which to show off the trophies and treasures that they had collected. It was filled with stuffed and mounted animals, footwear from around the world, and exotic forms of currency—and with whatever had struck the Morse family fancy. Nothing much had changed since the 1930s; no concession was made to changing political, social, or environmental attitudes. Like the Fairbanks, the Morse Museum was itself an exhibit, displaying an unsophisticated American view of a world that could still be regarded as fascinatingly exotic but of little real relevance to daily life. I shall miss it, and the America that one could see there.

An Evening with Richard Snelling

It's an election year, of course, and I try my best to be a responsible citizen. It's my aim never to miss an election, and never to cast an uninformed vote. Now, Vermont is a small state—third smallest in the Union, if population be your measure—and political life is lived on a reasonably small scale. With 150 members in our House of Representatives, each one has fewer than 3500 constituents. It would not be an impossible achievement for a representative to know, personally, every registered voter in his district. Anyone who is the least bit active in any social, professional, commercial, or religious organization is bound to meet state senators and executive officers in the normal course of business. And any Vermonter so reclusive as to escape these opportunities can meet all the politicians he wants at the statewide round of dinners, rallies, and forums that marks each campaign.

The local Republican organization put on a dinner last night at Hartford High School, practically just across the street from us. It was a pleasant night, and an inexpensive one: dinner was three dollars a plate, and the high school's culinary arts class acquitted themselves well. Most of the party's candidates for state office were present; the speaker was articulate and seemed very well informed; and the question period was notable for the high level of the discussion.

But for me the high point of the evening wasn't the speeches. One thing I've learned from attending my share of church dinners and chicken-pie suppers is that Vermonters are masters of the unexpected. The organic farmer sitting across the table may well be an Episcopalian priest when he's not in his fields; and the soft-spoken lady with the gray hair is as likely as not to be an expert on Chinese archaeology—*and* a powerful committee chairman in the state Senate. So I should not have been surprised at the unusual turn that the dinner-table conversation took.

A fellow at the next table (he was sitting less than six feet from me) mentioned that he'd been a frequent victim of mistaken identity, and began to wonder aloud if he had a double somewhere in the state, a man whose resemblance to him was so close as to make confusion inevitable. He then began to speculate on the use such a person might be to a harried politician. "That would be a good science fiction plot," he said. I told him that it had been done, citing *Double Star* and *The Star Beast;* and I asked if he read much science fiction.

I hadn't expected a wealthy businessman in a three-piece suit to be a science fiction reader. But I had underestimated Richard Snelling. As a child he had read the complete works of Edgar Rice Burroughs, and as a teenager included SF pulps among his favorite reading. (He credits science fiction with motivating him to overcome a severe childhood reading disability.) Ever since then Dick Snelling had read science fiction whenever he got the chance. We swapped book titles for a bit, and he asked me to write down a few suggestions. "I'll ask my wife to buy them for the kids for Christmas," he explained with a grin.

We talked for a bit about science fiction reading as preparation for a future of constant change, and when I used my favorite term "mental isometrics" to describe

SF's mind-stretching abilities, Snelling said that he'd used the same phrase himself. He particularly wanted to read more science fiction about politics, and agreed with my contention that a study comparing politicians who read science fiction with those who didn't would probably reveal some significant differences in outlook.

I'm afraid I must have monopolized much of Mr. Snelling's conversation: and his fellow diners at the head table probably didn't know quite what to make of our discussion. As an afterthought I asked him if he'd be receptive to an invitation to speak at a science fiction convention. He said that he would, time and geography permitting; but he'd want time to prepare a proper talk, with plenty of examples. I hope that the opportunity arises. He is an excellent speaker. And who might be better qualified to talk about "Science Fiction and Politics" than the outgoing chairman of the National Governors Association, the Hon. Richard Snelling, Governor of Vermont?

The Vermont Bicentennial

I can't understand why Vermont is celebrating its bicentennial in 1991. The celebration should properly have been held fourteen years ago. Vermont declared its independence in 1777, and joined the United States as the fourteenth state—the first addition to the thirteen colonies that signed the Declaration of Independence—in 1791. During those fourteen years, Vermont was what one historian has called a "reluctant republic." It sought admission to the United States in order to protect its citizens' land titles: New York, New Hampshire, and Massachusetts all claimed Vermont's territory as part of their own. As their land grants often overlapped, there was considerable conflict. Ethan Allen and his Green Mountain Boys held their property under grants from the governor of New Hampshire; their quarrel with New York sprang as much from their concern for the profits of land speculation as from their abhorrence of the feudal tenures then characteristic of York State landholdings.

Vermont's desire for admission to statehood was thwarted by New York; so Vermont proclaimed its independence at a convention in Windsor in 1777, and adopted "the laws of God and of Pennsylvania, until we shall have time to frame better." (The original idea had been to name the state New Connecticut, but nobody in Windsor knew how to spell it.) Historians are still trying to figure out the motives behind Ethan Allen's negotiations with the British during the Revolutionary War. Was he committed to American independence, or was he seeking the best environment for land speculation? Had Allen been offered a slightly better deal, I might be writing this in Canada's eleventh province today.

By 1791, New York had been persuaded to relinquish its claims on Vermont, a decision aided by the Green Mountain Boys' rough-and-ready treatment of York State surveyors and tax collectors. Vermont was admitted to the Union, and the two entities have got along tolerably well ever since. But the relationship has often been an ambivalent one; so it's not surprising that one of the activities sponsored by the Vermont Bicentennial Commission is a series of debates around the state on the resolution that Vermont ought to secede from the United States of America.

Arguing in favor of the resolution was Frank Bryan, co-author (with Bill Mares) of *Out! The Vermont Secession Book* (Shelburne, Vermont: The New England Press, 1987) and (with John McClaughry) of *The Vermont Papers: Recreating Democracy on a Human Scale* (Chelsea, Vermont: Chelsea Green Publishing Company, 1989). The former is a light-hearted exercise in political extrapolation, with as good a claim to being called science fiction as Allen Drury's *Advise and Consent,* which Sky Miller once reviewed in *Analog.* The latter is a serious argument for a reshaping of the American political culture, beginning in Vermont, where the state's low population and town-meeting tradition make small-scale participatory democracy a real possibility. Both books are written for Vermonters; both should interest many readers outside Vermont.

Out! takes as its starting-point the election of Alexander Haig to the presidency of the United States in 1988. Haig is one of the few political figures in the book that flatlanders will recognize; but almost every prominent Vermonter, politician or otherwise, appears either in his proper persona or in the thinnest of clever plastic disguises. Bryan and Mares are, of course, characters in their own book, playing properly heroic roles in The Ultimate Great War of Secession: it is Bryan who thwarts possible invasion from New York by pouring maple syrup into the gas tanks of American armored personnel carriers. But for all the tomfoolery, there is a note of wistful seriousness about *Out!* Most Vermonters, whatever their political persuasion, are convinced that Vermont is better run than the United States. That sentiment was far more powerful than left-wing sympathies in the recent election of Bernie Sanders, the independent socialist former mayor of Burlington, to Vermont's seat in the U.S. House of Representatives.

Bryan and Mares aren't the only ones who have dabbled in Vermont secessionist fantasy. David Hale offered "The Republic of Vermont: A Modest Proposal" in the *Northeast Kingdom Review* back in 1978; and in that same year, as part of a series of programs exploring the Quebec secessionist movement and its potential impact on Vermont, Vermont Public Radio broadcast "2001: A Vermont Odyssey." This was my contribution to the genre: a radio "pseudo-documentary" looking back, from ten years after independence, on the events that led Vermont to celebrate two hundred years as part of the United States by seceding from it. My approach was more solemn than that of Bryan and Mares; my precipitating factor was the election of Anita Bryant rather than Alexander Haig to the U.S. presidency; and my scenario owed more to economics than to sheer Vermont cussedness. But the basic idea was the same: Vermont could go it alone, and do a damn good job of it. I felt a small thrill of pride on the day it was broadcast, when I heard the narrator describe the setting of my little radio play: "Our nation's capital: Montpelier, Vermont." It was not solely the pride of authorship.

Vermont doesn't have to secede to enjoy a better political system. That's the message of *The Vermont Papers*, the product of two of Vermont's most stimulating political thinkers. Bryan and McClaughry draw their inspiration from a wide variety of sources. One chapter begins with a quotation from Ethan's firebrand brother Ira Allen; another begins with an excerpt from J. R. R. Tolkien's description of The Shire. The decentralization of government is their theme: devolution of state responsibilities to individual towns and to small groups of towns to be called shires, and—eventually—a universal devolution of national responsibilities to the local level, with Vermont serving as inspiration (and think-tank) to the world.

The history of utopian literature is replete with nationalist visions. I've run across titles from Ireland, Quebec, the Philippines, and more. At least one of these works, Theodor Herzl's *Altneuland,* can claim some influence in the creation of a nation-state. (It's ironic that Herzl's vision of a Zionist state in the land of Israel didn't foresee the revival of the Hebrew language. His Zionist utopia speaks German; in one touching scene, the traveler from a distant land who serves as our viewpoint character is taken to a school to see the children show off their ability to count to ten in Hebrew.) My inability to read Irish and Spanish will keep me from reading some of these books. Even the ones in English are hard to come by. (I've been trying for years to find the University of Toronto Press's translation of Tardival's *Pour la Patrie,* a novel of Quebec separatism from the mid-19th century.) But as a Vermonter I have a living branch of nationalist utopian literature right at hand, and I've even been able to make my own minor contribution to it. A few years ago a map called "Devolving Europe" displayed the new states that might emerge from the various separatist movements of that continent. Events in the Soviet Union and South Africa, as well as the changing role of national governments within the European Community, may well produce more nation-states than we can now anticipate. As a Vermonter I shall greet their emergence with interest, sympathy, and a little bit of envy.

A Bookman's Fantasy

The BBC used to have a program called "Desert Island Discs," on which a guest would be asked to name the twelve records he'd bring along were he exiled to a remote island. I'm sure I'd find books better companions in such an environment, and "A Desert Island Dozen" was my first try at selecting those I'd want with me. It appeared in *Lofgeornost* #1 (August 1979). I thought it would be a good way of introducing myself to the members of the Fantasy Amateur Press Association, which I had just joined: how better to know someone than to know his favorite books? Maybe sometime I'll have to have another crack at this. I imagine I've discovered a few more indispensable books in sixteen years.

One of my desert island books was *Silverlock*. I first encountered *Silverlock* during the summer of 1964, and upon reading it immediately understood why the book was so popular among the California fans from whom I learned of it. John Myers Myers wrote three stories in that one romance: an exciting adventure in a fantastic land; a *Bildungsroman*, but that of a man approaching middle age rather than an adolescent; and, most enticing of all, a most challenging literary guessing game. Over the course of several years Anne Braude and I managed to identify almost all of the allusions in Silverlock. The results of our research appear in "A Reader's Guide to the Commonwealth," part of *A Silverlock Companion: The Life and Works of John Myers Myers* (Center Harbor, New Hampshire: Niekas Publications, 1988).

Silverlock is one of those books whose reputation spreads by word of mouth. That I was successful in transmitting my own enthusiasm can be seen in "A Goliard Christmas," which appeared in *Niekas* #22 (1980). Perhaps it's just as well, though, that not everyone is susceptible to the book. Otherwise "A Day in the Commonwealth" might become a reality, and I don't think I'm ready for that. It originally appeared in *Niekas* #37 (August 1988).

A couple of years after I wrote "All Aboard!..."—it was published in *Niekas* #29 (February 1982)—I bought some HO-scale trains at a yard sale and set them up on a four-by-eight plywood board down cellar. Elizabeth and I named our line the Montpelier & White River; it's an entirely conventional model railroad layout. The Hobbiton & Michel Delving or the National Railway of Islandia would have been more of a challenge, but like the Vermont Commission on Tackiness some ideas are more sensible to contemplate than to execute. Still, I'd love to see what a really talented modeler could do with the concept ....

"Sherlock Holmes in India" originally appeared in *Lofgeornost* #8 (November 1986), but the hypothesis it proposes first occurred to me during my high school days twenty-five years before. I've long been an avid Kipling fan; I've also read the classic Irregular studies of the Sherlockian canon. So it was natural to explore the links between the two. I remember a Saturday afternoon spent reading Sherlockian publications in the New York Public Library, where all I found was a couple of brittle pamphlets linking Holmes to Strickland of the Indian police, a minor figure in some of Kipling's early Anglo-Indian tales. I like to think that I've discovered the *real* story behind the Great Game.

A Desert Island Dozen

The classic way to pose the question is this: "What books would you take with you to a desert island?" Let's limit the number to an even dozen. I don't expect to name all twelve of mine here. But I have a pretty good idea of what a few of them might be. I'll begin by saying that I have no intention of defining the Twelve Great Western Classics. My choices aren't meant to sum up anything so trivial as human civilization. They are much more, and much less, than that: they are the books that have shaped my thoughts in the past and will continue to shape them in the future.

Where to start?

Let's start with my favorite writer, for I'm certain of taking two of his books along. One of them will be *Rudyard Kipling's Verse: The Definitive Edition* and the other will be *Kim*. There are very few poets whose verse I can read, page after page, with anything like enjoyment. I'm reading some Robinson Jeffers these days, and several months ago I marveled my way through the poems of Gerard Manley Hopkins. But I can't think of any other poet I've been able to enjoy in large doses. Kipling's universality: his interest in *everything* that goes on in this world—his fascination with all her gaudy peoples and places—Kipling's straightforwardness, his ability to say what he is about in forceful, direct language; his joy in the good hard work of the world and his joy in the people who do it—these are the things that make Kipling a necessary part of my life; these are the warp and the woof of his verse.

And *Kim*? *Kim is* simply everything that is exotic in our world. *Kim is* the excitement of the Grand Trunk Road. *Kim is* the contemplation of the mystery of personality. *Kim is* a novel I have read a dozen times. Or is *Kim* a dozen novels each of which I've read just once? Ask me again after a year on the Island, and perhaps I'll be able to tell you which.

That's two of my twelve. Let me add a couple I've barely begun to taste. The *Collected Verse of Gerard Manley Hopkins* is a thin book; Hopkins died young, and his poems were published after he died. They were written almost a hundred years ago; they sound as if they were written today. They are like Möbius strips or Klein bottles, folded in upon themselves. Hopkins is as opposite to Kipling as English verse affords: perhaps on the Island I'd have the opportunity and the time to savor the difference between them.

I feel diffident about adding the works of Shakespeare to my list. Desert island bookshelves are littered with esteemed but unread books brought along, I suppose, out of a sense of duty—or perhaps to impress Friday should he happen along. But note, please: I'm leaving Montaigne and Milton and Spinoza at home on the Someday Shelf. Shakespeare is another matter. True, I've only read a few of the plays, and none of them as carefully as they deserve—but I know that I will, with a certainty that I cannot muster when I contemplate my shelves of other Great Writers. So I'll bring my *Complete Pelican Shakespeare* along.

I think I should bring along some joyous books. That means *Silverlock,* of course. As an adventure story it is superb. As a game it is unsurpassed. As an affirmation of what it is for a man to grow it is, quite simply, beautiful. And *Zorba the Greek* is another novel that I can turn to in confidence when my spirits want lifting.

And I'll take *Van Loon's Lives,* for the pleasure of their company. I don't mean the famous and infamous dinner-guests at Veere, but rather the companionship of Van Loon and his friend Frits and the ghost of Erasmus, drinking beer together on damp Dutch winter nights as the fog rolls in from the North Sea.

Friends together on a foggy night—yes, I'll have to bring along *The Complete Sherlock Holmes.* If ever a book was an endless well of pleasure it's this one; is there any other book that can bear so frequent re-reading? Has any other book inspired as joyous a band of scriveners and scholars? Whisky and soda-water and a winter's night—and the companionship, unseen though it be, of the Baker Street Irregulars. Remind me to tell you some time of my conjectures as to Holmes's activities after Reichenbach ....

Well, there are still some gaps on my Island bookshelf, but it's late, and I wouldn't miss my bedtime reading for anything. Let's leave the gaps unfilled for now. I'll not be visiting my Desert Island for quite a while, and I'd best leave room for books I discover or rediscover between now and then. I don't want to have to leave any behind.

A Goliard Christmas

I opened her letter. "I am sending you a present; unfortunately, it is all I can afford. It is a verse I discovered ...."

Boiling in my spirit's veins with fierce indignation,
From my bitterness of soul springs self revelation:
Framed am I of flimsy stuff, fit for levitation,
Like a thin leaf which the wind scatters from its station.

While it is the wise man's part....

There were twenty-five stanzas of it. "Does the scansion remind you of something?" Indeed it did: for Orpheus' Song from *Silverlock* has long been a favorite of mine. I first learned it thirteen years ago, when I heard Karen Anderson sing it, to a tune by (I believe) Bruce Pelz. And in my turn I taught it to several friends.

I have known both joy and grief, neat or mixed together;
Cold and heat I've known and found both good drinking weather;
Light and darkness I have known, seldom doubting whether
Tammuz would return again when he'd slipped his tether.

To Shandon Silverlock, the Commonwealth is a land of illusion. To the reader, it is a land of allusion; full of people and places and deeds and legends from all the histories and literatures of Earth. Now, I know that Orpheus' Song was a paraphrase (in six lively stanzas) of the *Epic of Gilgamesh*. And I knew that Orpheus was but one of O. Widsith Amergin Demodocus Boyan Taliesin Golias' myriad names—in fact Silverlock usually called him Golias. So I realized that Golias or Orpheus or whatever you'd like to call him was by way of being the Universal Bard. But it didn't occur to me that the allusion might go well beyond mere nomenclature. I should have realized...

The verses, she told me, were taken from a medieval history textbook, which in turn had reprinted them from John Addington Symonds' *Wine Women and Song*, a book of Goliard poetry. Like every well-educated young man I had heard of the Goliards: there was even one of their poems printed in my C.C. book, indicating that sometime during my freshman year I was supposed to have read the thing. Well, whether I read it or not, it obviously didn't take—else I would have identified Golias with the patron of the wandering medieval scholars who took the name of Goliards.

I determined to find out more. This is when it comes in handy to run a statewide interlibrary loan system. I looked up Symonds in the Vermont Union Catalog, and learned that *Wine Women and Song* contained translations of medieval student songs taken from the *Carmina Burana*, a Latin manuscript songster discovered in a German monastery and first published in 1847. I teletyped to Middlebury College for Symonds. A tracing on the catalog card led me to look up *Carmina Burana*, and I discovered that the University of Vermont owned a bilingual Latin-German edition. Again the teletype clattered.

I wanted to find the Latin original to the poem I'd been sent, and to see if its meter was the same; for I'm extremely fond of the tune, and of singing in languages I don't understand; and a medieval Latin drinking song would be a fine addition to my repertoire. But how would I tell which song in *Carmina Burana* was the right one? I haven't enough Latin for that, but I could probably find it through its German translation—and I could learn it in German as well.

When Middlebury's Symonds came in, I learned from it that my song was entitled "The Confession of Golias," and was ascribed to a probably nonexistent twelfth-century "Archpoet of Cologne." While I waited for UVM's *Carmina Burana* to arrive, I remembered my C.C. book, and in it I found this:

When through all the realms of earth "Go Ye Out" resounded,
Priests began to gad about, monks with rapture bounded,
Dreams from the Evangels rose, weary of redundance—
One and all our order join, seeking life's abundance.

This "Song of the Vagrant Order" is obviously another song entirely, though its sixteen stanzas fit the meter of "The Confession of Golias." I think I prefer its thoroughgoing impiety to the note of repentance with which "The Confession of Golias" ends.

I was thinking of all these things while straightening out my living room one day. I had come upon three paperbound Latin textbooks which I'd purchased last summer at a library booksale. Before taking them upstairs to their proper place in the lumber room, I sat down and flipped through them. And in the second volume of Sadler's *Modern Latin* I encountered:

Aestuans intrinsecus ira vehementi
In amaritudine loquor meae menti,
Factus de materia levis elementi
Folio sum similis de quo ludunt venti.

The twenty verses were entitled "The Confessions of Golias." The meter fits perfectly (only two elisions are required in the twenty stanzas!) and it has a marvelous sound to it. And when I get *Carmina Burana* I'll learn it in German too. And if I get a moderate amount to drink at some party, I'll sing it in Latin and German both.

Meanwhile, I've started reading some histories of the medieval universities; and I've decided that someday I'd like to write a story or two about the Goliard life. It's been a pretty exciting week, and it doesn't look like being over yet.

It may have been all she could afford. It was a damn fine Christmas present.

A Day in the Commonwealth

I've been working on *A Silverlock Companion* for years, and just because the project has been completed and the book finally published, I haven't lost interest in Silverlock. I hope that I haven't reached the point of obsession. But sometimes the most unlikely things will trigger an association with the novel.

The other day my five-year-old daughter received a postcard from Walt Disney World. My parents had been there, and they want us to join them there someday. I think that Elizabeth is a bit too young for that; and anyway, we have other priorities. My taste in fantasy lands runs more to Sturbridge Village or Mystic Seaport; and Sheryl and I have long-standing plans to return to Colonial Williamsburg, site of our honeymoon, for our tenth anniversary. Our little *tertium quid* will be just old enough for their children's programs by then. Walt Disney will have to wait.

Looking at the Disney World literature got me to imagining a theme park based on the Commonwealth. There's more to *Silverlock* than picaresque romance and literary allusion. John Myers Myers wrote a pretty fair adventure story: a lot happens to Silverlock and his friends on their journey. With a bit of imagination, a fair amount of technology, and a lot of money, the typical American family could be put through its paces by the Delian. So come with me as we spend a day at Commonwealth Park.

Our journey to the Commonwealth doesn't start off quite so adventurously as A. Clarence Shandon's. Instead of being lost overboard during a storm at sea, we wander an ocean of asphalt. Once we've found a parking place, there's the long trek to the gate. Nobody said that a day at a theme park was going to be easy. Or cheap. But the admission price covers everything save food, drink, and souvenirs. We have our passport to the Commonwealth, and all day to use it. Let's get going!

Once through the gate we find ourselves in Ilium, though everyone just calls it "The City." In the background stands the Arch King's Palace—it seems there are certain constants to the practice of theme park design. Nothing much happens in Ilium. Behind exotic façades stand prosaic vendors of T-shirts, photographic film, and suntan lotion. The Hell Fire Club houses nothing more diabolical than a Cajun-style fast food eatery. And the Fir Cone Tavern is just a glorified soda fountain. But as the crossroads of the Commonwealth, Ilium is an excellent starting point; and its streets and alleyways are a likely place to meet its more prominent citizens. We can use some of our film capturing Elizabeth sitting on Don Quixote's lap, or riding in Miss Kilmansegg's gilded sedan chair. (We'd do better to buy a picture postcard; but that wouldn't be in keeping with the theme park spirit, would it?) I wouldn't be too surprised to run into a few foreigners while we were about it. Distinctions aren't maintained too rigorously in these places, so I'd keep an eye out for such folk as Daunt Godolphin and Bobby Yare. Not to mention Doc Holliday, Jack Swilling, and the San Francisco Vigilantes!

But we didn't come here to spend the day mingling with hired help in costumes. We're here for adventure!

Where to start? Brodir Hardsark's Viking longship ride? The line's a short one, so we jump on board. Now we see why there wasn't much of a wait! This is no mechanical imitation of a longship. We're on those benches, three to an oar, and it's up to us to get the boat moving! Fortunately there's a bard on board, and we have a strong beat to time our oarstrokes. (The rowing is suspiciously easy work, and there's a funny noise from within the hull. Maybe our oars aren't telling the whole story.)

You can't see much from the oar deck of a Viking longship. Once ashore, it's a different story. The Battle of Clontarf is being fought in that little valley below us. It doesn't last long: ten minutes at the most. But if you want more, stick around. They fight it every half hour.

If cruising appeals to you, there are several more relaxing voyages available. A ride down Long River on Huck Finn's raft ('ware the steamboats!), or a short scenic journey on Lorel's barge, might be just the thing. And water's not the only path through the Commonwealth. If the sight of all those Houyhnhnms from Lorel's barge has awakened a fondness for horseflesh, you might want to try the pilgrimage to Hippocrene. But keep your wits about you—the leader might call on you for a song or story. If you're one of those barroom cowboys given to showing off on mechanical broncos, a ride on Avarta's nag ought to satisfy your cravings.

I know the ride I'd be most eager to try. I do the New Purchase Monorail every time I go. The backdrops are always changing, and lately there have been some exciting loops through some very strange stars and skies.

There's one ride that you must take. I've done it—once. You won't want to repeat it, I assure you. But you'll never be the same after that batwing tour of the Pit.

All this is getting a bit strenuous. Time to slow down a bit. How about a spot of lunch?

What's your pleasure? A venison on rye at Robin Hood's Deli? Steak and kidney pie, a tankard of ale, and a hot-blooded serving wench at the Inn at Upton? Or cock-a-leekie and haggis at Ambrose's Tavern—washed down with a dram of The Glenlivet? When I came out of the Pit I was feeling more than a bit queasy. All I wanted was toast and tea at the Night and Day Joint.

After lunch is a good time to relax and let our stomachs settle a bit. Take in a show, perhaps. Let's see. There's Hermione's wedding at the Chapel Perilous; that's always a fine spectacle. (And how *do* they manage that transformation scene?) Another treat for those who like special effects is Captain Face's Alchemical Demonstration. You won't believe what it takes to produce the Philosopher's Stone.

Or we could settle a few personal affairs. A visit to the Oracle might be rewarding, though it's much more likely to prove totally mystifying. The rules say that Deiphobe has to answer your question. But there's nothing that says that you have to be able to make sense of her answer.

For the ambitious self-improver, there's Piscator's Philosophical Academy and School of Fly Fishing, or the riding lessons at the Horse Farm. Too strenuous? Well, you can get through an afternoon's wine tasting at Ambrose's without straining anything but the elbow muscles.

A bit of shopping at the Parouart bazaar, and it's supper time. There are plenty of choices, but I always return to the same spot. The food and drink at Heorot are varied and substantial. Your fellows at table are always a hearty lot. And you can't beat the floor show.

I enjoy a lively sing-along as much as any man, and when the tables are cleared and the musicians appear, I trip a reel with the best of them. But the high point comes at the end of the evening. Returning to our seats for coffee, dessert, and brandy, we are serenaded by the finest bards of the Commonwealth. It's strictly individual performance, applause being the only audience participation. But I guarantee you'll be whistling a new tune for weeks afterward.

Then its back to Ilium for the fireworks, and time to leave. Good luck finding your car! You're no doubt weary of the whole business. Your kids, if they're still awake, want to come back again tomorrow. "Maybe next year," you tell them, not meaning a word of it. But when next summer rolls around, a repeat visit seems much more appealing. Some of the rides and attractions that left you cold last time make a lot more sense now. And you never know whom you'll meet there....

All Aboard! ...

I've long been a vicarious model railroader. When I was a boy I had a small, crude HO-scale layout in my parents' basement. It's been decades since I've had anything to do with model trains. Still, I rarely pass a hobby shop without spending a few minutes looking over its wares. I've told myself that the last thing I need is another indoor hobby: if I need to create a model environment, I should do so outdoors, with tulip bulbs and ornamental shrubbery. But I'm not entirely sure that I've convinced myself.

I've met modelers who have taken their prototypes from the railscape of Vermont. The covered bridge on the Lamoille Valley line, the circus trains that once visited Montpelier, the bustling railway-yards of White River Junction—there's a lot of Vermont's railroad history that's worth modeling. And not just its past: that covered bridge up in Wolcott is still in use, the only covered span on any American railroad; and a beautiful miniature steam locomotive still serves as weathervane on the White River depot. I've often thought that a diorama of Vermont railroading, past and present, would make an exciting exhibit; I once suggested the idea to the people at the Historical Society museum in Montpelier.

But I'd take a different tack myself. I'd take my prototypes from the imagination. I can think of at least three imaginary lands whose details have been carefully sketched out by their creators—all but their railway systems. And I would be tempted to make up that omission.

Once Meriadoc Brandybuck and Peregrin Took returned to the Shire from the War of the Ring, they would hardly spend the rest of their days sitting by their firesides. As Greathearts of the Shire, they would certainly be in demand at the Free Fair at Michel Delving; and surely their counsel would be sought by the King at Minas Tirith. Eagles may be indispensable in emergencies, but they can hardly be depended upon to serve as a rapid-transit system. A little steam-powered railroad—no massive, articulated behemoths (though I'd not be surprised to see a few rusting away amid the slag-heaps of Mordor, but rather friendly little pufferbellies—would be just the thing to link Hobbiton with Bree, or to start folk on their journey down the Greenway to Gondor.

Of course, any line serving Bree would need bimodal coaches: one half double-decked to carry large hobbit families, with rounded windows so that their passengers would feel at home, and the other half more spaciously furnished to accommodate men. The long-distance trains would doubtless have several types of accommodation, for elves and dwarves would have their own ideas of comfortable travel. Stations in the Shire would be of honest red brick, or perhaps fieldstone in hillier sections, rounded in the characteristic architectural style of the country, and would be surrounded by carefully-tended flower-gardens. The setting would be completed with model hobbit-holes, country inns with carefully lettered signboards, and figurines of small folk riding sturdy ponies.

A railway network in Middle Earth would hardly be restricted to the Shire. I can imagine an Elvish monorail gliding through the forest of Lothlorien, and a narrow-gauge underground line through the Mines of Moria. Try as I might, I can't picture a railway through Fangorn forest—the ents would hardly permit it—but I have no trouble visualizing orcish transportation: the comparison with the IRT at rush hour is too obvious. Perhaps I'd best stick to the hills and meadows of the Shire after all.

Another bucolic land needing improved transportation is Islandia. In Austin Tappan Wright's sprawling novel, land transport is limited to horses and wagons, while small sailing vessels link the coastal provinces. In *The Islar*, Mark Saxton's sequel to *Islandia*, we learn of the new monorail line, linking the Islandian capital ("The City"), the university town of Reeves, and the border region of The Frays. Presumably a monorail would be less disruptive of the Islandian way of life than would be a more conventional railway; Islandians seem to have learned how to integrate the twentieth century into their traditional culture. But it would still seem characteristic of the place for a network of meter-gauge country railways to carry a mixed traffic into the hinterland of Storn and Winder. (And what a picture The City's Union Terminal would make!)

Which brings up the possibility that Islandia's railways wouldn't be nearly as interesting to the modeler as the country itself. Austin Wright was an avid amateur naturalist, and careful descriptions of topography and wildlife abound in his novel. (Much of the material cut when his voluminous manuscript was prepared for publication dealt with Islandian geology.) While the sketch-maps he drew are difficult to read (especially in the Signet paperback edition), Wright's word-pictures of Islandian farmsteads and townships give a vivid portrayal of a distinctive landscape. And The City, with its brightly colored buildings, its network of roof gardens and skyways, and the variegated fleet of two-masted coastwise sailing ships crowding its harbor, would be a marvelous challenge to the imaginative modeler.

The rural branch line with its daily mixed train is the sort of thing most modelers have in mind when they create their idealized portraits of American railroading. And where would such a picture be more appropriate than in that archetypal middle-American small town—Lake Wobegon, Minnesota? Any regular listener to "A Prairie Home Companion" knows the names of Lake Wobegon's landmarks: Skoglund's Five and Dime, Ralph's Pretty Good Grocery, the Chatterbox Cafe. The very name of the Side-Track Tap implies the existence of a railway line through the village.

I like to think of the Minneapolis & Lake Wobegon as a home-town effort at preserving rail service on a never-prosperous branch of some overbuilt granger road. The same train that hauls a couple of boxcars of Powdermilk Biscuits might carry the Sons of Canute to a lodge convention in the Twin Cities, or start Barbara Bunsen on her way to another term at the University of Minnesota. But I'll concede that I might be wrong in picturing it as a steam railroad. The M&LW might be an impecunious interurban line, with big dark-green cars rumbling along Main Street in front of the green mobile home housing Bob's Bank, or wobbling through Norwegian bachelor farmers' wheat fields as it makes its way toward St. Cloud. It might even have degenerated into a sort of Toonerville trolley, bringing crowds in its rickety cars on still summer nights out to the old Wally "Hard Hands" Bunsen Memorial Field to see the Whippets play.

I may yet come back from a hobby shop with an Ambroid "One in Five Thousand" kit and a few lengths of Atlas SnapTrack. But don't expect my cellar to sprout any clone of the Boston & Maine: there are more fitting tracks to be laid by a fantasy fan.

Sherlock Holmes in India

More than twenty years ago, I realized that a well-known book, usually regarded as an adventure story for boys, was in fact an oblique account of Sherlock Holmes's activities during the "missing years." The Canon tells us little of Holmes from the time of his carefully-faked death at the Reichenbach Falls until his return to London ("The Adventure of the Empty House"). We have Holmes's own brief resume of those years:

> I travelled for two years in Tibet...and amused myself by visiting Lhassa, and spending some days with the head lama. You may have read of the remarkable explorations of a Norwegian named Sigerson, but I am sure that it never occurred to you that you were receiving news of your friend. I then passed through Persia, looked in at Mecca, and paid a short but interesting visit to the Khalifa at Khartoum, the results of which I have communicated to the Foreign Office .... ("The Adventure of the Empty House")

In *Sherlock Holmes of Baker Street*, W. S. Baring-Gould suggests that Holmes spent at least part of that time in Montenegro, where he begat Nero Wolfe upon Irene Adler. Perhaps he did; I fancy there isn't all that much else to do in Montenegro. But it is my conviction that Holmes was up to something rather more important.

Now, my knowledge of Sherlockian historiography is sadly out of date. The idea I put forward here was original thinking in 1962, when I conceived it; and in a private letter Baring-Gould himself affirmed its plausibility. But it may well be that in the past twenty years some other Sherlockian has happened across the same document that I did; or perhaps the Sherlockian consensus has fixed upon an alternative chronology of the missing years. Still I find my hypothesis an attractive one; and here it is:

Holmes never told Watson the true reason for his absence from London. The whole episode at Reichenbach was merely a cover for some work he was doing for the Foreign Office, at the urgent request of his brother Mycroft. ("You would also be right in a sense if you said that occasionally he *is* the British government."—"The Adventure of the Bruce-Partington Plans") And what was it that so concerned Mycroft Holmes and the Foreign Office? Nothing less than the security of the Indian Empire.

For the Russians had designs on India, and were attempting to bring nearby Persia, Afghanistan, and Tibet into their sphere of influence. The Indian Army was fully capable of repulsing any military attack; but some subtler agency was needed to undo the damage caused by Russian spies and infiltrators. Such an agency existed. To outsiders, it was an innocent research bureau of the Government of India. But the staff of the Ethnographic Survey knew that their real mission was the security of the Empire. And, thanks to Rudyard Kipling, we know of some of the moves and countermoves in their Great Game.

I haven't the space here to retell *Kim;* all I can do is urge anyone who hasn't read the book to do so. (I doubt that I'll have to urge anyone who *has* read *Kim* to re-read it.) Let us assume at least a nodding acquaintance with its plot, and proceed to ask some questions.

Why did the Teshoo Lama leave his monastery in the hills of Tibet? We're told that he had learned of Western research into Buddhist lore that narrowed the location of the River of the Arrow, which brings salvation to him who bathes therein. And from whom did he learn of this? Perhaps from "a Norwegian named Sigerson."

When Kim was judged ready for advanced training in The Great Game, he was sent to the "healer of sick jewels," a Eurasian called Lurgan, who kept a shop in Simla. Lurgan was a master of disguise, a close student of comparative human behavior, and a man whose powers of concentration and persuasion bordered on the supernatural. We are told that he was well above average height. Haven't we met such a man before—on Baker Street?

And what of Billy, "the young but very wise and tactful page" ("The Adventure of the Mazarin Stone"), of whom we hear nothing elsewhere in the Canon? Kipling tells us of the extraordinary impression which young Kim made upon "Lurgan." Would not a postgraduate course at the Baker Street campus be an invaluable part of a young operative's training?

There are—as always in Sherlockian studies—a few trifling problems with the chronology. But ascribing these to Watsonian discretion (or to Watsonian carelessness!) lies well within the permissible techniques of Sherlockian historiography.

I should like to hear from Sherlockians whether my conjectures seem reasonable, and whether they have been anticipated or superseded. In the meantime, I nominate *Kim* as the fifth Sherlock Holmes novel.